FROM
T
MOTION PICTURE

Peter Hyams to Arthur C. Clarke (January 19, 1984)

A PACKAGE HAS JUST BEEN MAILED TO YOU . . . A MINOR ITEM CALLED THE SCREENPLAY. MORE THAN ANYTHING ELSE I HAVE TRIED DESPERATELY TO PRESERVE YOUR VISION AND CONCEPT . . . WHILE MAKING THE ALTERATIONS THAT ARE NECESSARY TO TURN A BOOK INTO A FILM. I USE THE TERM "ALTERATIONS" INTENTIONALLY. THIS IS YOUR SUIT, OF YOUR DESIGN. I AM NOTHING MORE THAN A TAILOR . . . TRYING TO FIT IT TO A DIFFERENT BODY. I HOPE YOU ARE PLEASED WITH WHAT YOU READ. NEXT CHRISTMAS . . . IF YOU AND STANLEY [KUBRICK] ARE NOT EMBARRASSED BY WHAT YOU SEE . . . I WILL NOT HAVE WASTED TWO YEARS OF MY LIFE.

∞   ∞   ∞   ∞

Arthur C. Clarke to Peter Hyams (February 6, 1984)

Nice timing, Peter, the screenplay arrived this morning . . . I felt like playing a few tricks on you--like a message from my secretary saying that I was last seen heading for the airport carrying a gun. But given the delicate condition you are in, I'll say right away that it's a splendid job and you have brilliantly chiseled out the basic element of the plot, besides adding quite a few of your own. I laughed--and cried--in all the right places.

∞   ∞   ∞   ∞

Peter Hyams to Arthur C. Clarke (February 7, 1984)

I CANNOT BEGIN TO TELL YOU HOW YOUR RESPONSE MADE ME FEEL. I AM GRATEFUL AND A BIT MORE THAN RELIEVED. THIS IS THE MOST CHERISHED MOMENT I HAVE HAD SINCE I SAID I WAS FOOLISH ENOUGH TO DO THIS FILM. I THANK YOU.

THE ODYSSEY FILE

Arthur C. Clarke

Author of the novel *2010: Odyssey Two*

and

Peter Hyams

Screenwriter-Director of the movie *2010*

A Del Rey Book

BALLANTINE BOOKS • NEW YORK

A Del Rey Book
Published by Ballantine Books

Copyright © 1984 by Serendib B.V., Peter Hyams Productions, Inc. and MGM/UA Home Entertainment Group, Inc.

Cover and interior illustrations copyright © 1984 by MGM/UA Entertainment Co.

All rights reserved under International and Pan-American Copyright Conventions. Published in the United States by Ballantine Books, a division of Random House, Inc., New York, and simultaneously in Canada by Random House of Canada Limited, Toronto.

Library of Congress Catalog Card Number: 84-90939

ISBN 0-345-32108-1

Manufactured in the United States of America

First Edition: January 1985

Editing and expurgating by Steven Jongeward
Stunts and Special Effects by Jonathan Zimbert and
Gerard Raymond
Computers by Kaypro
Modems by Hayes Microcomputer Products, Inc.
MITE Communications Protocol by Mycroft Labs, Inc.
WordStar by Micropro
Printers by Epson
Circuits by Intelsat
Phone Bills picked up by MGM/UA

CONTENTS

INTRODUCTION

ELECTRONIC LIFE

MOUNTED ON A WOODEN PLAQUE IN MY TV LOUNGE is a piece of armored cable about half an inch in diameter and four inches long. It is, frankly, not a very glamorous object, and you would be surprised to learn that Tiffany's went to the trouble of acquiring it in 1858. Slightly more than a century later it was presented to me by Ambassador Abbott Washburn, United States negotiator at the conferences setting up Intelsat—the world communications satellite organization.

Given these clues, you might be able to guess that it is a section from the first transatlantic submarine telegraph cable, which ushered in the age of global telecommunications. There it sits, this triumph of Victorian high technology—the nineteenth-century equivalent of the Apollo Project—underneath the monitor on which I watch TV programs beamed down from the satellites in stationary orbit 22,000 miles above my head . . .

Between the crudely made cable and the fifteen-foot TVRO dish on my roof lie a hundred years of engineering science. Yet in the last *ten* years another almost equally great communications revolution has taken place; without it, this book would have been not only impossible but inconceivable.

When *2001: A Space Odyssey* burst upon the hapless world, back in 1968, I defended myself against those who demanded a sequel by pointing out that such a thing was out of the question because (a) I won't leave Sri Lanka for more than a few days; (b) Stanley Kubrick absolutely refuses to set foot in one of these newfangled flying machines. Little did I imagine how quickly this argument would be demolished by the onrushing wave of communications technology.

Still less did I imagine how soon that same technology would transform my own lifestyle by converting into everyday reality what once seemed predictions about a remote future. It is a reality which at the moment is shared by perhaps a few hundred thousands in the developed countries—predominantly the United States—but which will spread swiftly throughout the world.* Perhaps the best label for this new technology is "electronic mail"; but that gives about as much idea of its ultimate potential as the now-obsolete word "wireless" did for the possibilities of electromagnetic wave communication when it was first used in 1894.

1894? That's what the great *Oxford English Dictionary* says, giving as proof an astonishing quotation

---

* For more details, see the essay "Beyond the Global Village" in *1984: Spring* (Ballantine, 1984).

from the *Westminster Gazette* for 22 February of that year: "Man may be able some day to communicate by wireless telephone with the planets . . ."

Good for the *Westminster Gazette*—but it overlooked one important point. We can send anything we like between the planets and far beyond them. (Pioneer 10's signals are still being received, even though it has already passed the orbit of Neptune.) But telephony—meaning real-time conversation—will never be possible to the planets because of the limiting velocity of light. Even the two-and-a-half-second time lag on the round-trip between Earth and Moon is quite annoying; and who would hang on the line for six minutes to get an answer back from Mars, even at its closest?

Yet a delay of six minutes is perfectly acceptable—indeed, often welcome!—when one is dealing not with spoken words but with printed text. The familiar cablegram and its successor the telex were the first signposts on the road which has led to the systems of electronic mail that are now embracing the world. Let me tell you how I got plugged into the global network.

It all began with my first microcomputer(s). Since I can never resist glamorous technological toys, I had lusted after a personal computer as soon as they came on the market in the late seventies—though I had no idea what I would use one for.* I had seen a few video games, had heard talk of something called "word processing," and felt that it might be fun to play with both. So I read everything I could find on the subject and waylaid any experts who passed

---

* For the full story of my love affair with computers, see "HAL Jr. versus the Integers" in *Ascent to Orbit* (Wiley, 1984).

through Colombo. One happened to be Steve ("Woz") Wozniak, the inventor of the Apple, who came to Sri Lanka for his honeymoon (and later sent me a musical Christmas card which terrified the postman, as it was already performing when it arrived). Another was Richard Bock of Business Computing International, New York, who persuaded me that video graphics and word processing didn't mix very well and I needed a separate machine for each. This is no longer true, but in the far-off days of 1981, Richard's advice was sound and I've never regretted buying an Apple II for fun and games, and an Archives III for serious work. (Not, of course, that the Apple can't be used for both.)

At this point, I have a problem which cannot be solved by an Apple, an Archives, or even a CRAY. A large but unknown percentage of you, dear readers, will have forgotten more about the care and feeding of computers than I shall ever know; so I must apologize for the ensuing baby talk. At the same time I must beg the forgiveness of the still larger percentage who wouldn't know a REM from a ROM, or a floppy disk from an interface, and who are just as confused by computer jargon as I was in—oh, let's say 1980. I can assure them that it is amazing how quickly and relatively painlessly one picks it up—just as an earlier generation effortlessly added to its vocabulary such exotic words as ignition, accelerator, high octane, compression, spark plug, gearshift, clutch . . . which would have been totally baffling to its grandparents.

For the benefit of computer virgins, if such there still be, let me say briefly that the Archives III* which

---

* The Archives series is no longer in production, so I'm not getting a penny for this. However, I would like to say that "Archie" has given

is swallowing up these words even as I type (and frequently mistype) them stores text on two separate, spinning magnetic disks. One (the hard disk) is sealed in the machine and can hold the equivalent of a million words, or approximately ten novels. The other (the floppy disk) can hold about one novel or a dozen short stories—or several hundred letters—or any mixture of these. The floppy, which looks much like a 45-rpm record, can be removed from its drive unit; so a whole library of disks can be built up, devoted to different subjects ("files") or programs—just as one can collect music or sound recordings on tape cassettes. (Indeed, the familiar audio cassettes are often used as cheap—but painfully slow—storage devices for computers.)

There would be no point in all this hardware if the machine—let's not call it a computer, for the operations we are now considering have nothing to do with mathematics—merely displayed text in luminous letters on a TV-type screen. The final product usually needed is still old-fashioned print on paper—or hard copy, as it is called in the trade.

When Archie entered my life in late 1981, I was about a quarter of the way into *2010: Odyssey Two* and had already produced about a hundred sheets of messy manuscript on my electric typewriter (I wonder where that is now? It must be *somewhere* round the house . . .). As soon as I realized what word processing could do, all writing came to an abrupt halt. I was in exactly the same position as an Egyptian scribe who had spent his life carving inscriptions on granite—and suddenly discovered ink and papyrus.

---

me trouble-free service for two years, and if he blew up tomorrow he would have paid for himself fifty times over.

Again, my apologies to those who were already saving files on disk when I was still writing my last-but-one last novel, back in the seventies. Please skip the next few paragraphs.

Quite simply, word processing removes the sheer drudgery from writing, thereby vastly increasing output *and improving quality*. I am not going to waste time arguing about this and turning myself into that dread literary-cocktail-party menace, the Word Processing Bore. Let me instead quote one of my favorite book titles: *Shut Up, He Explained.*

However, I am prepared to admit that there are cases where word processors may not be the best tools; but not very many of us have an exclusive output of sonnets, which of course can be written only with quill pens.*

As soon as I discovered that the WordStar program enabled me to make instant corrections, shift blocks of text around and join them seamlessly, automatically locate any given words or phrases within seconds in a twenty-page article, justify or unjustify margins, etc., etc., I was converted. Perhaps what really appealed to me was the total abolition of carbon paper; from now on, *every* manuscript would be

---

* The only author I ever met who actually used a quill pen was Lord Dunsany. I have in front of me at this moment my autographed copy of *The Charwoman's Shadow*, which he insisted on correcting on pages 338 and 339, changing the word "Towards" to "Beyond," and I can almost swear that he blotted it with sand instead of paper. Perhaps if he had composed on a word processor, the most perfect ending in the whole of fantasy would have existed in more copies than mine:

And now for him, and the creatures that followed after, the gates were wide that led through the earthward rampart of the Country Beyond Moon's Rising. He limped towards it with all his magical following. He went therein, and the Golden Age was over.

an original. When I needed extras, I would put the appropriate floppy disk into the drive—and read a book or listen to music while perfect, errorless copy rolled out of the printer.

So I hired local talent to load the raw first 25 percent of my original typescript into Archie's capacious memory, and then carried on from there, writing directly on the machine. I can honestly say that I have never touched a typewriter since that day.

Nevertheless, I was still using Archie as little more than a super typewriter, for the final result was identical with that which could have been produced by an immaculate typist. There was one important difference: I did not send a thick pile of paper to New York, but airmailed a thin, strong envelope containing a single floppy disk (after, needless to say, making a duplicate with the machine's COPY command—an operation which took only a few minutes). The printing-out of the manuscript from the disk took place in New York; theoretically, the publisher could have set the book directly from the disk, thus eliminating the later chore of proofreading—the most onerous duty of every conscientious author.

Obviously, if a whole book can be encoded in the form of magnetic pulses on a disk, there is no need to send the actual disk *physically* to the desired destination. The pulses can be sent over a telephone or radio link, and received on any suitable computing system at the other end. But not until *2010* was already in New York, and I had had the inevitable second thoughts, did I begin to exploit this possibility.

Doing so required a small black box known as a modem (for modulator-demodulator) connecting Archie to the international telephone circuit. It also required a special program (itself stored on a floppy disk) to tell him how to manipulate the material being transmitted, so that it would make sense at the other end. ("Begin new line; start next page; indent new para here; underline from this letter; *stop* underlining after this letter"... as well as many other instructions that a human typist, not being a literal-minded high-speed idiot, takes for granted.)

It was a great thrill when, after several false tries, I succeeded in sending a short file called ODYCOR from Colombo to New York. The final words of the Acknowledgments record this historic event: "Last-minute corrections were transmitted through the Padukka Earth Station and the Indian Ocean Intelsat V."

And that was that for more than a year; although the experiment had worked, I had no further use for the facility. Indeed, I was more than a little worried by the breach I had made in my hard-won isolation. What if those persistent New York editors realized that articles could now reach them in seven minutes instead of seven days? A horrid thought ...

The situation changed abruptly in late 1983, when MGM/UA commissioned Peter Hyams to write the screenplay and make the movie. I remembered with nostalgic affection my three years with Stanley Kubrick,* and though I certainly no longer had the time or the energy for collaboration on such a scale, it might be fun to see what could be done with the new electronic facilities. Moreover, I did have a certain responsibility in the matter, and would like to know just what was going on in Culver City, California ....

But this time, thanks to the new technology, I would be in complete control of the situation. Sitting

---

* See *The Lost Worlds of 2001* (New American Library, 1972).

quietly in my Colombo home I could do as much or as little work as I liked. I knew nothing about Peter Hyams (though I had been quite impressed by his previous films *Capricorn One* and *Outland,* despite certain reservations), and if I didn't like the guy, I could always pull the plug on him.

So Peter and I started looking at the available systems, and shortly thereafter I received news that a Kaypro II was on the way to me.

This was slightly embarrassing, as my good friends at IBM had just presented me with their elegant new PC; moreover, I would have to learn yet another operating system. But it did not take long to master the Kaypro; all personal computers are basically the same, though unfortunately most of them speak different languages and refuse to talk to one another. The main problem was that I had grown so used to Archie's excellent keyboard that I have never been able to use any other without making at least one mistake per line.

Along with the Kaypro came a Hayes Smartmodem, which the telecommunications department connected to my international direct dial telephone while I tried to make sense of the book of instructions. Peter was doing the same in Los Angeles; but *he* had the advantage of being able to consult the local experts while he struggled up the learning curve. And here I would like to give thanks to Jim Swanner and Dave Rothman, who spent a great deal of time patiently teaching us how to use the system, particularly the MITE software that controlled it.

The experience was frustrating but fun—rather like learning to ride a bicycle by reading a book of instructions that explained precisely what every muscle had to do. Like most computer documentation, the relevant brochures were written in a language which, though it bore a striking resemblance to English, often managed to convey no information whatsoever.

Although I made every possible mistake in the early days (to the great profit of the telecommunications authorities involved), after a few weeks the operation of the system became automatic and effortless. Eventually I found I could no longer even *deliberately* produce some of the disasters I had once created at the keyboard. (I still haven't solved the Case of the Evaporating Dialogue Files.)

Our first attempts at communication were not unlike those of the Atlantic cable pioneers a century and a quarter earlier. I can claim to be an authority on this subject, since one of my most carefully researched, and financially unsuccessful, books, was devoted to it.* Thus an entire *day's* traffic on the very first (1858) cable consisted of fifteen short phrases like "Repeat, please"; "How?"; "Please send slower"; "Can you read this?" and a despairing "Please send something."

Peter and I managed a little better than this, and my first complete message to him consists of a couple of hundred words, dated 83 September 16. It ends with this prophetic paragraph: "Do you realize we may have a book here?! We'd better, to pay the phone bill."

Peter's first to me, the next day, is somewhat shorter. Here it is *in toto*:

THIS IS A TEST FILE. IT IS OF NO REDEMTIVE OR EDUCA-
TIONAL VALUE. YOUR LIFE WILL NOT BE ENHANCED BY

---

* *Voice Across the Sea* (1958). I don't even know if it's still in print.

READING IT. THIS IS SIMPLY AN ATTEMPT TO SEND A FILE
THROUGH THIS SILLY PILE OF METAL AND PLASTIC. I RE-
MAIN YOUR HUMBLE SERVANT AND FAN. HYAMS.

After a few false starts, some of which now make
hilarious reading, we worked out a standard operating procedure which took care of the most important
single factor in our situation—the difference in time
zones. Peter and I were almost on opposite sides of
the globe; he was eight hours behind Greenwich—I
was five hours thirty minutes ahead, giving a total difference of thirteen hours and thirty minutes west-
wards, or ten hours and thirty minutes eastwards. (I
have been campaigning against that stupid and ut-
terly pointless thirty minutes for years. Only a dozen
countries have nonintegral time zones, which play
havoc with international phone calls and airline
schedules. I am happy to say that as a result of my
persistent agitation the Sri Lanka Cabinet has finally
decided to put the country six hours ahead of Greenwich: we hope that our big northern neighbor India
will go along with us.)

It followed, therefore, that we were almost a hundred and eighty degrees out of phase; one of us was
usually asleep while the other was working, and vice
versa. But with electronic mail, this doesn't matter.
One can use it as a "time shifter"—as video cassette
recorders are now used in millions of homes to re-
schedule TV programs at more convenient viewing
hours.

At first I used to leave my machine switched on
during the night, set in ANSWER mode so that it could
receive anything Peter wanted to send while I was
sleeping. But this didn't work, for a reason that nei-

ther of us had anticipated. Though I could get through to Los Angeles in ten seconds, it sometimes took Peter hours to reach Colombo; when he appealed in desperation to his friendly local operator, he was liable to be told that there was no such place as Sri Lanka.

So eventually we settled down to a routine in which I did all the dialing from my end. This is how it now works:

When I get up in the morning, I switch on my machine and tell it to call Peter's office number, which it knows and dials automatically—no small chore, since thirteen digits and one letter are involved, starting with p001 213 ... No, I won't give Peter's modem number.

His machine (unless the MGM security guard has accidentally knocked out the power plug or kicked the modem in a vital part of its anatomy) is already waiting in ANSWER mode and flashes back a message which means "Here I am: what do you want me to do?"

I then take charge, just as if I were sitting at the keyboard in Culver City, and ask it to list all the files that are stored in its No. 2 floppy disk, designated B. (The other disk—A—carries all the commands for word processing and communications: B is reserved purely for our correspondence, and is replaced by a new disk when it is full. Each disk can hold 64 separate entries, or about 40,000 words. The later Kaypros have many times this rather modest capacity.)

Peter's machine then swiftly lists the names of all its current files, and displays them to me in numerical order: "PH49   PH50   PH51 ..." I look at the last entry and see if it's a new number—in other words, a file I've not already received. If it is, I type "SEND B:PH51," tell my own machine "RECV PH51," and sit back while the file comes through. It takes about a minute—two dollars of phone time—for a page of double-spaced text to be transmitted. (Much faster and cheaper rates are possible, on circuits of good enough quality, but we have been playing it safe.)

In this particular mode, I can't actually read the file as it's coming across, but have to wait until it has all been safely stored on my B disk. When I get the signal FILE RECEIVED I hang up promptly, and then tell my machine to display the message. Then I usually edit it, correcting Peter's grammar and spelling (though he's now getting quite good at "*i* before *e*"). Often some garbage has been picked up—odd letters and weird computalk symbols that have escaped from the machines' own private conversations. I zap all these with the DELETE key, and when I'm satisfied get a printout of the immaculate, electronically blue-penciled result.

During the day I brood over my reply, and load it on to my B disk at convenient moments. Just before I go to bed (I seldom make it to the 9:30 TV news—which is 8:00 A.M. in Los Angeles) I once again tell my machine to call Peter's, but reverse the SEND and RECV instructions. When my file has been transmitted, I usually double-check by looking at his directory (i.e. list of files) to see that the new number is there. At the moment, I'm up to AC155; he's only reached PH72.

This is not because I am twice as garrulous as Peter, but because our daily exchanges stopped abruptly as soon as shooting began and he was occupied more than full time on the set.* By then, anyway, the screenplay had been completed and the various technical problems worked out; there was little more useful input that I could provide as far as the movie itself was concerned. But because I have now become an addict and need my regular fix of news and gossip from the studio, I still go on-line every day and exchange files with our joint assistant Steven Jongeward, who is now manning the bridge as far as communications are concerned.

Steven is also doing a great deal more than this, because he is copying disks, printing out files, and generally handling all the mechanics of the operation—much of it on his own Kaypro in his spare time during the smaller hours of the morning. I don't know when he sleeps, because he opens up the production office round 7:00 A.M. Los Angeles time, and is still at the studio when I go on-line twelve hours later to see what messages are in the machine for me.

I know he's there, because when I have downloaded the incoming file I type

hi

and wait. Within a couple of seconds there is usually something like

HELLO THERE IT'S ME STEVEN I LEFT AROUND 11:30 AND I'M STILL WAKING UP

This demonstrates the other major usage of the system—its ability not merely to exchange docu-

---

* Editorial note: In order to have this book in the stores when the film of *2010* is released, the published correspondence ends at PH72.

ments but also to conduct *real-time* conversations just as fast as we can type. What is even more important, these conversations—like the regular files—can be saved, edited, and printed out to be reread at leisure.

And they certainly need to be edited, because neither Steve nor I qualify as high-speed precision typists, and the raw material is full of mistakes, abbreviations (remember, this is costing two bucks a minute, so we try not to waste time) and occasional mysterious hieroglyphs from outer space. To make clear who's talking to whom—not always obvious when reading the printouts days or weeks later— Steve uses CAPITALS while I employ lower case. (Like archie—the cockroach, not the computer.)

You might imagine that all this hardware and the rigid protocols necessary to operate it would make all communication totally impersonal. Indeed, I half expected that at the beginning, but I should have known better. After all, only two years earlier I had feared that creative writing would be impossible on a word processor, whereas the exact opposite turned out to be the case.

Once I had learned its operation, the system I was using vanished from my field of consciousness. (In computer jargon, it became transparent.) This was particularly striking in my dealings with Peter Hyams; though I had never met him and didn't even know what he looked like, we very soon became old friends, trading jokes and insults in the files we exchanged, and even more so in our real-time dialogues. Perhaps the most unexpected development of all was that, after some thirty years of purely business correspondence, I found myself writing chatty *letters* again, full of random musings, accounts of local ac-

tivities, and similar matters of not the slightest re-
deeming social value. It may have been the excite-
ment of playing with a new toy, or the stimulus
provided by virtually instantaneous feedback from
the other side of the globe; whatever the explanation,
I became a regular electronic gossip—at least until
the call of duty dragged Peter away from the console
and he had no time to reciprocate.

One could easily become addicted to this new
video vice, thanks to the computer networks and data
bases* that are springing up all over the planet. Some
of my friends tried to introduce me to one of the
many electronic noticeboards on which one can leave
or read messages, but I soon decided that enough was
enough. Even talking to a single terminal was length-
ening my working day by at least an hour, and the
prospect of becoming accessible to thousands of ad-
ditional global villagers was simply too appalling to
contemplate. Perhaps when I am too senile for any
other form of activity, I may start babbling of green
fields over the computer networks.

I have, however, taken one cautious step toward
extending my electronic correspondence by installing
a Kaypro in my English office so that brother Fred
(who handles my European affairs and maintains the
Clarkives) can get in touch with me instantly. To
spare him—and my staff here in Colombo—the diffi-
culties I had faced, I started writing a brief guide to
the communications protocol. Even if it tells you
more than you want to know about the subject, a

---

* The *OMNI On-line Database Directory* (Macmillan, 1983) is an excellent introduction to these fascinating new tools, which will soon be
playing an even greater role in business and social life than has the
telephone for the last hundred years.

quick glance at my hitherto unpublished thesis, "MITE for Morons,"* will give you the flavor of this marvelous new technology. You might as well start here; sooner or later you will have to learn how to use it.†

As I type these words on Archie's keyboard, late at night here in Colombo, today's file is already stored in a billion microscopic magnets on the current B disk. In a few minutes I will type SEND, and my Kaypro will start relaying B:AC156 by cable and satellite to its twin in Peter Hyams' office at MGM. And in exactly a week's time I shall be following it, at a slightly lower speed.

Soon I shall be meeting an old friend for the first time. I wonder if we'll still like each other.

—Arthur C. Clarke
Colombo, Sri Lanka
April 15, 1984

---

* This appears as Appendix Two.
† Steven's latest dispatch informs me that there is a new and much improved version of MITE waiting for me in Los Angeles. I hope it does not differ too greatly from the program in which I have invested so much blood, sweat, and tears.

THE ODYSSEY FILE

This is the first attempt to send a file from Colombo to L.A.

William Sylvester (Dr Floyd in "2001") phoned recently from L.A. and talked at some length--but I'm not clear if he was after his old role or not (he said he was semi-retired). You might contact him.

I'm impressed by the Daily Variety spread sent by Steve. But Leonov* is

---

* The spaceship in *2010: Odyssey Two*, named after Cosmonaut General Alexei Leonov, the first man to do a space walk and also commander of the USSR spacecraft during the Apollo-Soyuz linkup. *2010: Odyssey Two* is dedicated to him and to Academician Andrei Sakharov. For an account of my last meeting with Alexei, see "To Russia with Love" in *1984: Spring*.

crazy--as shown, it couldn't possibly fold up behind an aerospace
shield. Incidentally the authority
on this subject is M Cruz (JPL D-
691), who's edited a monumental report on Aerocapture dated May 83. I
sent you a letter of his a few weeks
ago. After it's dumped its shield,
of course Leonov can open up as much
as it likes.

Incidentally it's so far cost me
about $900 to clear this machine,
get it repaired (it simply refused
to switch on), and I haven't yet had
the bill from the teams of high-
priced software experts in permanent residence. . . .

When you tried to call, only two of
the six incoming circuits were
operating--trouble on Pacific
cable, not comsats! OK now . . .

All my files will have the name
B:MGMn so you will always know what
to ask for when you download from me,
and will also know if you missed any.
I suggest you call yours ACC(n) in
the same way. Do you realise we may
have a book here?! (We'd better, to
pay the phone bill.) End of MGM1.

DEAR ARTHUR:

THIS IS A TEST FILE. IT IS OF NO REDEMTIVE OR EDUCA-
TIONAL VALUE. YOUR LIFE WILL NOT BE ENHANCED BY
READING IT. THIS IS SIMPLY AN ATTEMPT TO SEND A FILE
THROUGH THIS SILLY PILE OF METAL AND PLASTIC. I RE-
MAIN YOUR HUMBLE SERVANT AND FAN.

HYAMS.

PH4. SEPTEMBER 22, 1983

DEAR ARTHUR:

LOS ANGELES IS BECOMING MILDEWED. ALL OF THE TROPI-
CAL HUMIDITY THAT OCCURS ONLY IN OTHER AREAS HAS
BEEN SENT HERE BY JEALOUS CHAMBERS OF COMMERCE.
THE LARGEST SOUND STAGE IN AMERICA IS BEING SWEPT
CLEAN BY TATTOOED MEN IN BASEBALL HATS . . . IN PREP-
ARATION FOR THE CONSTRUCTION OF THE LEONOV. IF ALL
GOES WELL . . . FOUR MONTHS AND GOD KNOWS HOW
MANY MILLIONS OF DOLLARS FROM NOW . . . YOUR
SPACECRAFT WILL SPUTTER TO LIFE. (IF THE HAND CRANK
WORKS.)

THE POD:

IN THE DISCOVERY . . . THERE IS ONE POD LEFT. WHEN A
CLOSE INSPECTION OF THE MONOLITH IS NECESSITATED
. . . THIS IS THE VEHICLE THAT IS USED.

PLEASE THINK THIS THROUGH WITH ME. WE ARE GOING TO
SPEND ALL THE TIME, MONEY, AND EFFORT ON A MISSION.
THE MISSION IS TO GO UP TO JUPITER . . . RENDEZVOUS
WITH THE DISCOVERY . . . BOARD IT . . . AND THEN TAKE
A CLOSE LOOK AT THE MONOLITH. WE ARE BUILDING A
SPACECRAFT FOR THIS MISSION. WE DON'T KNOW WHAT

CONDITION DISCOVERY IS IN. IT COULD BE AILING. IT COULD
BE DEAD . . . BEYOND HELP. IT COULD BE DAMAGED. IT
COULD BE WRECKED. IT COULD BE FINE.

I AM NOT SURE WE WOULD PREDICATE A CLOSE INSPEC-
TION OF THE MONOLITH ON THE PROBABILITY OF A POD
REMAINING IN DISCOVERY. WE WOULDN'T KNOW IF IT WAS
THERE. WE WOULDN'T KNOW IF IT WAS IN WORKING CON-
DITION, EVEN IF ONE WAS THERE.

I THINK THAT LEONOV SHOULD HAVE ITS OWN PODS . . .
OF A DIFFERENT DESIGN. I THINK THAT THE CLOSE INSPEC-
TION OF THE MONOLITH SHOULD BE DONE WITH ONE OF
THESE VEHICLES.

ACC6 of 23 Sept 83

Your pod query. See p. 124, lines 4-
5. Probably Leonov would have its
own pods too but wouldn't risk using
them on this first recce when Discovery's was available and ex-
pendable. However, for dramatic
purposes it might be best to have the
first inspection a manned one, and
if a Russian goes out it would be
sensible to use his familiar machine. The Americans would use Discovery's. Use whichever option you
think best scriptwise.

PH8. SEPTEMBER 23, 1983

I DELIVERED YOUR MESSAGE TO DR. ROSEN.* HE WANTS
YOU TO KNOW THAT HE IS FINALLY STARTING TO WORK ON
A SPACE STATION. IT IS MORE LIKE 2001 THAN NASA'S
PLAN. HE SAID THAT IN THE CURRENT ISSUE OF SCIENCE
'83, THERE IS A PHOTOGRAPH OF NASA'S CURRENT
SPACE STATION . . . UNDER THE CAPTION: "2001 IT'S
NOT." NASA'S PLAN IS NOT TO PROVIDE GRAVITY. HIS
PLAN IS MUCH MORE LIKE 2001 . . . HE ALSO IS DESIGN-
ING A "DUAL SPIN" SYSTEM . . . SOMETHING HE SAID YOU
KNOW A GREAT DEAL ABOUT. HE ADDED THAT HE WAS
GOING TO BRING ABOUT A RENAISSANCE OF THE 2001
SPACE STATION IDEA . . . AND HE WANTED YOU TO KNOW
THAT HE FELT THERE WAS A "GOOD CHANCE" IT WOULD
ACTUALLY COME ABOUT. HE ALSO SAID THAT HE WOULD
LIKE TO TALK TO YOU. I GAVE HIM YOUR TELEPHONE NUM-
BERS. I ASSUME THAT YOU WOULD NOT MIND.

PH8, PAGE 2:

AS SOON AS I AM A BIT FARTHER DOWN THE LINE . . . I
WILL SEND YOU SOME DRAWINGS OF THE DESIGNS. I AM
NOT SURE IF I WILL HAVE TO PUT MY FLAK VEST ON . . .
CONSIDERING YOUR RESPONSE TO THE FIRST DRAWING I
SENT TO YOU. AS FAR AS CASTING GOES . . . I HAVE NOT
MADE ANY CHOICES YET. I NEED MORE OF THE SCRIPT TO
GET A BETTER FEEL FOR WHO IS THE BEST CHOICE FOR
THE VARIOUS ROLES. OF COURSE I WILL TELL YOU WHO I
AM THINKING OF.

---

* Dr. Harold Rosen, pioneer of space communications and vice president of Hughes Space Division. His team was responsible for the
launching of the first stationary satellites, and has built most of those
orbited since.

PH9. SEPTEMBER 22, 1983

YOU MAY BE INTERESTED TO KNOW ABOUT HOW I AM
GOING TO MAKE JUPITER. YOU DO REALIZE, OF COURSE,
THAT YOU WROTE A STORY THAT TAKES PLACE IN PROBA-
BLY THE MOST DIFFICULT LOCATION TO RE-CREATE IMAG-
INABLE. YOUR DESCRIPTIONS ARE MAJESTIC. HOWEVER
. . . IT IS ONE THING TO WRITE ABOUT WHAT JUPITER
LOOKS LIKE. IT IS ANOTHER THING TO TRY TO PUT IT ON
FILM. MY GOAL IS TO PRODUCE THE MOST ACCURATE AND
DETAILED IMAGE OF JUPITER EVER PUT ON FILM. IF MY
TECHNIQUE PROVES SUCCESSFUL . . . WE WILL HAVE A
BETTER MOVING IMAGE THAN JPL.* WORKING WITH JPL
. . . I AM USING A MAN WHO IS A PIONEER IN COMPUTER-
GENERATED IMAGERY AND HAS A CRAY† SUPERCOM-
PUTER. IN FOUR WEEKS . . . HE IS GETTING THE NEWER
VERSION . . . WHICH IS THE MOST POWERFUL COMPUTER
IN THE WORLD, NOT OWNED BY THE GOVERNMENT. WE
ARE USING JPL PHOTOGRAPHS, AND TURBULENCE MAPS
THAT ARE ACCURATE TO 100 METERS . . . AND WE ARE
CREATING AN ANALOGUE THAT WILL REPRODUCE ALL OF
THE CURRENTS, ALTITUDES, AND MOTION OF EVERY
CLOUD FORMATION ON THE SURFACE. IT WILL COST ABOUT
THREE QUARTERS OF A MILLION DOLLARS . . . HAS NEVER
BEEN ATTEMPTED BEFORE . . . . IS PROBABLY FOOLISH . . .
AND JUST MIGHT PRODUCE THE MOST STARTLING IMAGE

---

* The Jet Propulsion Laboratory, Pasadena, California, has been responsible for most of the United States' scientific spacecraft program—especially the fantastically successful Voyagers to Jupiter and
Saturn, without which *2010: Odyssey Two* could not have been written. At this moment (May 1984) the Galileo spacecraft, which hopefully will survey the moons of Jupiter in the fall of 1988, is residing in
the JPL assembly room. I have just had the opportunity of examining
the machine, which if all goes well will visit most of the places described in the novel.
† The CRAY-1 is one of the world's most powerful supercom-
puters—at least at the time of writing.

ANYONE HAS EVER SEEN. SOME OF THE INITIAL TEST RESULTS ARE ENCOURAGING.

A LITTLE MORE ON THE LEONOV DESIGN . . . THE ONE YOU LOVED SO MUCH. I HAVE DESIGNED A LIVING SECTION . . . SOMEWHERE CLOSE TO AMIDSHIPS . . . THAT SPINS. I WANTED LEONOV TO LOOK COMPLETELY DIFFERENT THAN ANY SPACECRAFT PREVIOUSLY FILMED. I ALSO WANTED TO HAVE AN ARTICULATED SPACECRAFT . . . TO MAKE IT LOOK LESS LIKE A GIANT PEICE OF PLASTIC. I WORKED WITH JPL ON THE IDEA. THEY AGREED THAT IT IS NOT ONLY FEASIBLE . . . IT IS THE MOST LOGICAL DESIGN THEY HAD EVER SEEN. I COINCIDENTLY SPOKE WITH YOUR DR. ROSEN AT HUGHES ABOUT IT TODAY . . . AND HE SAID THAT IT WOULD BE ABSOLUTELY NECESSARY TO PROVIDE GRAVITY ON A MISSION OF THAT LENGTH. HE SAID THAT BESIDES THE SERIOUS DECALCIFICATION THAT OCCURS IN PROLONGED PERIODS OF WEIGHTLESSNESS . . . IT WOULD BE IMPOSSIBLE TO WORK IN A WEIGHTLESS ENVIRONMENT AFTER A WHILE. I TOLD HIM THE DIMENSIONS . . . AND HE CONFIRMED THAT THEY WERE PERFECT.

ACC3 of 24 Sept 83 rev 26 Sept.

Delighted you contacted Hal Rosen and even happier that he is designing space stations. Look forward to hearing from him live or on MITE. Ask him what happened to the guy who told Steve and me 24 Nov 82 on our way to L.A. airport that there was no role for man in space.

But he could be right. Since the Shuttle toilet has failed eight times out of eight, someone up there may be trying to tell us something.

There is a picture of a "dual spin" space station in my "Going into Space" (Harper, 1954, yes '54!), possibly available in the Rare Book Section of the Library of Congress.

I'm way ahead of you on Son of Hal: that's one reason I'm instantly WordStarring and printing out our immortal prose. When it's all over our executors will have a complete book and need only edit the material and correct your iddio idyio idiosyncratic spelling. Since you will also be accumulating printouts, it can be continuously edited from your end and would be ready about the same time as the movie.

Your Jupiter plans sound marvellous. I knew about the new JPL Super Cray setup, and there are several angles that occur to my tiny but active mind. What you commission should also be of scientific value, which would create goodwill in NASA and the beleaguered astronomical community. It will also focus interest on Galileo, which needs all the help it can get.

And then at the appropriate time you can fix a red eye on the Super Cray and take some publicity pix.

PH10. SEPTEMBER 26, 1983

MY DISCUSSIONS WITH JPL ABOUT THE SPACECRAFT RE-
SULTED IN THE SAME CONCLUSIONS. IT IS EASIER AND
MORE PRACTICAL TO CONSTRUCT A HEAT SHIELD . . .
THAN TO FOLD A SPACECRAFT. ONE HAS ONLY TO
PROJECT THE ANGLE OF THE CONE TO FIND HOW GREAT
AN AREA BEHIND IT IS SHIELDED. I ALSO DESIGNED A
SLIGHT OUTWARD LIP ON THE SHIELD . . . WHICH PRO-
VIDES A WIDER AREA OF DEFLECTION. THERE SEEMED TO
BE UNANIMITY ON THIS SUBJECT.

PLEASE CONSIDER MY SPELLING A SOURCE OF AMUSE-
MENT, NOT ANNOYANCE. WHEN I FIRST STARTED IN THIS
BUSINESS . . . TWELVE YEARS AGO . . . MY FIRST
SCREENPLAY WAS ENTITLED "T. R. BASKIN." I MADE THE
FILM AT PARAMOUNT. IT STARRED CANDICE BERGEN,
JAMES CAAN, AND PETER BOYLE. ABOUT TWO MONTHS
BEFORE SHOOTING STARTED . . . I SENT THE SCRIPT TO
MY MOTHER. SHE CALLED ME ONE DAY . . . AND IN AN AL-
MOST REVERENT VOICE . . . SHE SAID THAT IT WAS BEAU-
TIFUL . . . SHE WAS OVERWHELMED. NOW FOR MY
MOTHER TO DELIVER UNQUALIFIED PRAISE TO ME . . . THIS
IS NOT AN EVERYDAY EVENT. I WAS STUNNED. THEN SHE
SAID . . . "THERE WAS NOT A WORD MISSPELLED . . .
NOT ONE." I TOLD HER THAT I WROTE THE SCRIPT . . . I
DIDN'T TYPE IT . . . PARAMOUNT HAD NICE LADIES WHO
TYPE FOR A LIVING. THERE WAS AN ENDLESS PAUSE ON
THE PHONE . . . WHERE YOU COULD HEAR THE HISS OF
THE LONG-DISTANCE TRANSMISSION . . . AND SHE THEN
HUNG UP.

PH11. SEPTEMBER 27, 1983

I WAS UNABLE TO GET THROUGH TO YOU TODAY. I TRIED
USING OPERATORS . . . I TRIED DIALING DIRECT . . . I

TRIED CUPPING MY HANDS AND SHOUTING TOWARDS THE
PACIFIC. NOTHING SEEMED TO WORK. OPERATORS HERE
MUST FLUNK AN I.Q. TEST BEFORE THEY ARE ACCEPTED BY
THE TELEPHONE COMPANY. I DID MANAGE TO HAVE ONE
OPERATOR GET THROUGH TO THE COLOMBO OPERATOR
. . . ONLY TO HAVE THE COLOMBO OPERATOR SAY THAT
YOUR LINE WAS BUSY. I FEEL LIKE PETER SELLERS IN
STANLEY'S* "DR. STRANGELOVE" . . . FINDING THE RE-
CALL CODE THAT WILL SAVE THE WORLD . . . AND UNABLE
TO CALL THE PRESIDENT BECAUSE HE DIDN'T HAVE A DIME
. . . AND HE DID HAVE A DUMB OPERATOR. IT IS NOW 7:00
IN THE EVENING. I HATE ALL OPERATORS. I HATE TELE-
PHONES.

ACC11 of 28 Sept

Just had a very amusing letter from
Jorge Luiz Calife.† Will send it to
you; he asks what happened to the
models etc. on 2001 (all destroyed,
alas--Stanley told me that some twit
at Borehamwood decided they weren't
worth the storage space) and quips:
"Coming soon: 'Raiders of the Lost
Props.' "

Will send this off now at 9:15 a.m.
your time and will stay up for an-

---

* Stanley Kubrick, as if you hadn't guessed, was of course the pro-
ducer/director of *2001: A Space Odyssey*, and has already made his
name as one of the world's greatest moviemakers, with *Dr. Strangelove*, *Paths of Glory*, etc.
† The ingenious and well-informed Brazilian fan whose letters
started me thinking seriously about *Odyssey Two*. See acknowledgments in the book.

```
other thirty minutes if you want a
shoulder to weep on in real time.
Best--Arthur.
```

PH14. SEPTEMBER 29, 1983

I DIDN'T READ ABOUT RAIN IN THE LOST ANGELES BRO-
CHURES. THEY SHOWED PHOTOGRAPHS OF PALM TREES
. . . AND BLOND LADIES . . . AND BRIGHT BLUE SKY. THE
PALM TREES ARE HERE . . . THE BLOND LADIES HAVE
SUSPICIOUSLY DARK ROOTS . . . AND SOMEBODY TOOK
THE BLUE SKY AWAY. IT'S RAINING AGAIN. REAL RAIN. THE
KIND THAT IS SUPPOSED TO FALL ON OTHER CITIES. ALL
THE METEOROLOGISTS ARE SMILING IN FRONT OF THEIR
MAPS . . . AND EXPLAINING THAT WE ARE IN THE START OF
A NEW WEATHER CYCLE FOR SOUTHERN CALIFORNIA. I
PAID FOR THE OLD ONE . . . THE ONE WITH THE SUNSHINE.

I KNOW THIS IS OF CRUCIAL IMPORTANCE TO YOU. THE
DODGERS ARE CLOSE TO WINNING THE PENNANT. HOW-
EVER, IF IT KEEPS RAINING, THEIR GAMES MIGHT BE CAN-
CELED . . . AND THAT COULD HURT THEM. I AM RELAYING
THIS INFORMATION BECAUSE I AM SURE YOU ARE UNABLE
TO START YOUR DAY'S WORK WITHOUT KNOWING HOW
THE DODGERS ARE DOING. THE DODGERS, IN CASE YOU
DIDN'T KNOW, ARE THE GREATEST BASEBALL TEAM IN THE
WORLD. BASEBALL, IN CASE YOU DIDN'T KNOW, IS LIKE
MACHO CRICKET. YOU WILL BE THE ONLY PERSON IN SRI
LANKA THIS WEEKEND WHO IS ARMED WITH THE KNOWL-
EDGE THAT THE DODGERS ARE THREE GAMES IN FRONT OF
ATLANTA . . . WITH THREE GAMES TO PLAY. IT SHOULD
MAKE YOU A HIT AT PARTIES.

THE PHYSICAL LINKUP BETWEEN LEONOV AND DISCOVERY:
I AM A LITTLE FOGGY ON ONE POINT. I KNOW IT IS IN THE

BOOK . . . IT IS PROBABLY THE RAIN ON MY HEAD THAT'S
CAUSING MY CONFUSION. WE PULL AWAY FROM IO BEFORE
WE LINK THE TWO SPACECRAFT, FOR OBVIOUS REASONS.
THEN WE PERFORM THE LINKUP. THEN DO WE TRAVEL
CLOSER TO THE MONOLITH? IF WE DO . . . DO WE DETACH
THE SPACECRAFT AND THEN RE-ATTACH? OR . . . AM I
COUNTING ONE TRIP TOO MANY. DO WE JUST PULL AWAY
FROM IO . . . ATTACH THE TWO . . . AND SEND OUR POD
TO THE MONOLITH FROM THERE.

I APOLOGIZE FOR SOUNDING SO DENSE. THE ANSWERS
ARE PROBABLY SO OBVIOUS THAT THESE QUESTIONS WILL
ONLY SERVE TO MAKE YOU MORE APPREHENSIVE ABOUT
THE INCOMPETENT DIRECTOR WHO IS IN THE PROCESS OF
BUTCHERING YOUR NOVEL.

I WILL TURN THE MACHINE OFF AFTER SENDING THIS. I WILL
SLITHER BACK INTO YOUR B DISK MONDAY MORNING MY
TIME TO GET MY ANSWER. HAVE A GOOD WEEKEND. THINK
OF THE DODGERS. I WILL CONCENTRATE LESS ON THEM
. . . AND MORE ON 2010, I PROMISE.

ACC13 of 30 Sept 83

I've got a good title for our correspondence. How about *The Odyssey
File?* Oh well, it was a nice try . . .

Obviously I could do a lot without
much hassle when I come over in April
for the Marconi Award Ceremony,
though I wonder if the date will have
to be changed in view of the President's China trip. It would be fun to
talk wandering round the sets. (But

beware: see "Lost Worlds of 2001,"
top p. 39—attention Syd Mead.*)
Meanwhile I will be happy to continue my daily scoldings, as I am a
born yentor (masculine of yenta;
invented by Harlan Ellison†). Have a
good weekend: I'll remain on ANS tonight and may even be awake to about
9:30 a.m. your time if you want any
quick reactions. I'll switch off for
the w.e. until your Monday morning.

ACC14 of 3 Oct 83

S'matter of fact I agree with you
about cricket and have often made
friends and influenced people here
by quoting a Yankee description of
it as the slowest form of animal
life. However, I have never had the
slightest interest in any sport except table tennis (not, repeat not
ping-pong), which is my only other
recreation and which I play reli-
giously two hours a day at a local
club 4 to 6 p.m.

I think it's implicit on p. 127 that
the ships were not coupled until

---

* One of the most talented in the now very wide field of science fiction illustrators, Syd Mead's work has been seen in *Blade Runner* as
well as many other movies.
† The now-middle-aged enfant terrible of American science fiction—and one of the best writers in the business. He is equally well
known as an anthologist (e.g., see his *Dangerous Visions* series).

they reached their final 5 km distance after two earlier pauses at
100 and 50 km (pp. 120-122). However, I see no objection if for dramatic reasons and to tighten story
line you omit earlier stops and go
straight to the final location,
doing the pod survey too from this
distance if indeed you want to keep
that. I assume that by 2001 space-
ships will have at least one standard docking hatch on the lines
pioneered by Apollo-Soyuz, which
incidentally was captained by
Alexei.*

I have at last started again on the
new novel† after over a month and
feel quite happy about it. But sin-
ister forces are at work waving lots
of green paper to get me involved in
"Odyssey III," which I don't even
want to think about until the Galileo flyby at the end of the decade.

Hope it's stopped raining. Makes a
nice change from earthquakes anyway.

PH15. OCTOBER 3, 1983

IN THE FIRST PLACE . . . TABLE TENNIS IS A GAME WHERE
EXTREMELY SHORT PEOPLE WITH TINY RACKETS PLAY

---

* Alexei Leonov. See note on page 3.
† *Songs of a Distant Earth.*

TENNIS ON TOP OF A TABLE. PING-PONG IS A GAME WHERE REGULAR-SIZED PEOPLE HIT A LITTLE WHITE PLASTIC BALL WITH PADDLES. THE VAST MAJORITY OF THEM HAPPEN TO BE ORIENTAL, AND QUITE SERIOUS. SECONDLY . . . THERE ARE TWO TYPES OF YANKEES. THE MOST IMPORTANT GROUP . . . IS A COLLECTION OF BASEBALL PLAYERS WHO WORK IN NEW YORK. THE OTHER GROUP IS ALL AMERI-CANS . . . MOST OFTEN REFERRED TO WITH THE SUFFIX "IMPERIALISTS." MOST OF THEM CAN'T HIT.

CONSTRUCTION STARTED TODAY. THE LEONOV IS NOW A SERIES OF BLUEPRINTS AND VERY CONFUSED CAR-PENTERS. IN FOUR MONTHS . . . IT WILL BE EITHER ONE OF THE TRULY IMPRESSIVE SETS IN FILM HISTORY . . . OR A SERIES OF BLUEPRINTS AND VERY CONFUSED CAR-PENTERS. WITH ALL OF THE MONEY THEY GET . . . THEY WILL BE A BUNCH OF CONFUSED AND DEAD CARPENTERS.

THE SUN CAME OUT OVER THE WEEKEND. THE DODGERS WON. THIS IS A GOOD OMEN. GOD IS SMILING ON LOS AN-GELES.

PH16. OCTOBER 3, 1983

I BELIEVE YOUR INSTINCTS ARE CORRECT. I WILL MAKE ONE STOP AND THEN LINK UP. I HAVE NO PREFERENCE BE-TWEEN THE 50 OR 100 KM DISTANCE FROM THE MONO-LITH. IF ONE MAKES MORE SENSE THAN THE OTHER TO YOU . . . PLEASE TELL ME.

I AM WORKING WITH SYD MEAD AND JPL ON THE PHYSICAL LINK. I AM NOT SURE IF IT SHOULD BE ONE THAT IS EN-CLOSED. I REALIZE THAT BY ENCLOSING THE LINK, ONE DOES AWAY WITH THE NEED FOR ENVIRONMENT SUITS . . . HOWEVER, THERE ARE TWO PROBLEMS. ONE . . . IS A

DREADFUL TELEVISION MOVIE THAT USED A LONG FLEXI-
BLE TUBE TO LINK TWO SPACECRAFT. IT LOOKED A LOT
LIKE A VACUUM HOSE. IT WAS THE ONLY DECENT EFFECT. I
CAN'T DO ANYTHING THAT EVEN REMOTELY RESEMBLES
SOMETHING THAT WAS ALREADY ON TELEVISION. TWO . . .
ALL OF US BELIEVE THAT WHATEVER MECHANISM LINKS
THE TWO SPACECRAFT SHOULD NOT REQUIRE PEOPLE TO
WALK. THIS WOULD CAUSE ENORMOUS FATIGUE . . . AND
WOULD MAKE THE TRANSPORTING OF ANY EQUIPMENT
EVEN MORE DIFFICULT. ALSO WALKING ON ANY KIND OF
FLEXIBLE SURFACE WOULD MAKE THE JOURNEY MUCH
MORE OF A PROBLEM. I KNOW I SAID THERE WERE TWO
REASONS. HERE IS THE THIRD: I WANT TO MAKE THIS LOOK
HAZARDOUS. I FEEL THAT IF THE MECHANISM EXPOSED
THE ASTRONAUTS TO SPACE . . . IT WOULD BE VISUALLY
MORE EXCITING. WHAT WE HAVE COME UP WITH IS SOME-
THING ON THE ORDER OF A SKI TOW. IT IS A TRIANGLE OF
CABLES . . . TWO AT THE TOP AND ONE AT THE BOTTOM.
SUSPENDED BETWEEN THE TWO TOP CABLES IS A TRACK
AND TOW BAR. EVERY FIVE METERS . . . THERE IS A THICK
METAL TRIANGLE THAT SUPPORTS THE WHOLE THING. THE
ASTRONAUT (COSMONAUT) STANDS ON A T-BAR . . . AND
OPERATES THE TOW. THERE ARE TWO NINE-FOOT CIRCU-
LAR AFFAIRS THAT FIT OVER THE HATCHES OF EACH
SPACECRAFT. I DESIGNED A NINE-FOOT HATCH FOR THE
LEONOV . . . BECAUSE WE MEASURED DISCOVERY'S . . .
AND IT IS NINE FEET. IT SEEMED LOGICAL THAT THERE
WOULD BE A STANDARD SIZE BY THEN. I WILL SEND YOU
THE DRAWINGS WHEN SYD COMPLETES THEM. I WILL ALSO
SEND YOU THE BRIDGE DRAWINGS. I HOPE YOU WILL
AGREE THAT NO ONE HAS SEEN THIS KIND OF DESIGN IN A
FILM DEALING WITH SPACE. IT IS USELESS TO TRY TO DE-
SCRIBE IT. YOU WILL SEE IT. YOU MUST PROMISE, HOW-
EVER . . . THAT NO ONE . . . ABSOLUTELY NO ONE . . .
SEES THESE DRAWINGS. I AM TOTALLY PARANOID ABOUT
THIS. EVERY SCIENCE FICTION MAGAZINE IS DYING TO GET
THEIR HANDS ON A DESIGN FROM 2010. IT WOULD BE ON

THEIR NEXT COVER IF THEY DID. I HAVE TAKEN SECURITY MEASURES THAT ARE EXTREME TO SAY THE LEAST. THE STAGES ARE LOCKED . . . AND GUARDED. NO ONE IS ALLOWED ON WITHOUT IDENTIFICATION BADGES. THE ART DEPARTMENT IS LOCKED. NO DRAWING HAS LEFT MY OFFICE. SO PLEASE . . . ACCEPT MY CRAZINESS FOR WHAT IT IS . . . PARTIALLY BASED ON GOOD JUDGMENT. I WILL SEND YOU THESE DRAWINGS BECAUSE THEY ARE BASED ON YOUR HEART AND YOUR WONDERFUL IMAGINATION . . . AND YOU DESERVE TO SEE THEM.

AS FAR AS ODYSSEY III GOES . . . IF THEY PAY YOU TO SAY YOU WILL WRITE IT . . . THEN SAY YOU WILL WRITE IT. IF THEY ARE PAYING YOU TO ACTUALLY WRITE IT . . . THEN THAT'S ANOTHER STORY.

ACC15 of 4 Oct 83 02.30gmt

Some quick comments--the whole idea of the link was to save suiting up, which is a frightful chore. However, you could combine your mechanism rather nicely with the Shuttle rescue ball to give something like the elevators inside the Atlanta Hyatt-- very pretty, though maybe too much like Shelley Winters et al. in "Towering Inferno."

I promise to burn your drawings etc. before looking at them and know exactly what you mean. Probably Starlog* already has us bugged.

---

* *Starlog* magazine—the monthly magazine that covers the fields of science fiction, movies, TV, video games, etc. Its publisher, Kerry O'Quinn, will appear later in these pages.

PH17. OCTOBER 7, 1983

WE ARE ONE FULL WEEK INTO SET CONSTRUCTION. ASIDE
FROM THE ACTUAL BUILDING OF THE LEONOV . . . WE ARE
ALSO MAKING EVERY SWITCH AND EVERY GAUGE TO MY
SPECIFICATIONS AND SYD MEAD'S DRAWINGS. THEN
EVERYTHING HAS TO BE WIRED . . . SO THAT EVERY
SWITCH WORKS ON ITS OWN . . . AND HAS ITS OWN LIGHT
SOURCE. THIS MOVIE IS GOING TO COST HUNDREDS OF
DOLLARS.

I JUST RECIEVED YOUR MOTHER'S BOOK* YESTERDAY. I
READ IT LAST NIGHT. IT IS CLEAR THAT YOUR INTELLI-
GENCE IS NOT A GENETIC ACCIDENT. FOR YOUR INFORMA-
TION . . . I KNEW WHAT I WAS UP AGAINST BEFORE I READ
THE BOOK.

THE ONLY THING MY MOTHER EVER WROTE . . . WAS A
RECIPE FOR CHOPPED CHICKEN LIVER . . . AND THAT WAS
ON THE BACK OF A PAPER BAG.

GET SOME REST . . . AND HAVE A GOOD WEEKEND.

ACC18 of 83 Oct 10 1600 GMT

Thanks for PH 17. I too am delighted
to get my daily fix of bytes, as I was
beginning to suffer from withdrawal
symptoms.

---

* *My Four Feet on the Ground* was a collection of my mother's remi-
niscences, which we persuaded her to put together in her eighties,
which was published by my English company, the Rocket Publishing
Company. The preface I wrote to it may be found in *1984: Spring*.

Some waffling before I get down to business.

George and Darla Mueller* had a nice trip across the island to our east coast diving village and are now on their way to Budapest for the International Astronautical Federation Convention. I ran the London IAF in 1951 and am happy to sit this one out, especially as I should miss too many lost friends.

Incidentally, George and Deke Slayton† went over the "2001" sets in 1964, and Roger Caras‡ (whom you must contact) put out the story that they said, "Stanley, you've been conned by a used capsule salesman."

After having had no high-level assistance for six months I hope to have an Executive Secretary cum Deputy starting this week. He's an ex-Ambassador, engineer, and first-rate artist--and built the space-station model for Stanley in '64!

---

* Dr. George Mueller, deputy administrator at NASA during the Gemini and Apollo programs and therefore the man largely responsible for the success of these tremendous undertakings.
† D. K. Slayton, astronaut, was one of the original Mercury Seven, but was unable to fly on the space program for some two decades because of a slight heart condition. He finally made it with the Apollo-Soyuz mission.
‡ Stanley Kubrick's vice president in charge of publicity on *2001: A Space Odyssey*. Author of many books on wildlife and natural history and well known for his radio programs on this subject.

PH18. OCTOBER 10, 1983

YOU MUST UNDERSTAND THAT TO BE JEWISH AND GUILTY IS TO BE REDUNDANT. MY GRANDMOTHER TOLD PERFECT STRANGERS THAT SHE HAD NOTHING TO DO WITH THE DEATH OF CHRIST . . . AND WENT AS FAR AS TO FURNISH HER ALIBI . . . (SHE WAS IN THE LOBBY OF A DIPLOMAT HOTEL IN MIAMI BEACH WITH FOUR FRIENDS AT THE TIME IT HAPPENED.) I AM NOW SIEZED WITH THE HORRIBLE IMAGE OF THIS SYMPHONY OF BEEPS AND RINGS, ECHOING THROUGH YOUR OPEN DOOR AT OBSCENE HOURS OF THE NIGHT. I AM HUNCHED OVER THIS LITTLE MACHINE . . . WATCHING DOTS AND RRRRRRRRS AND TTTTTTTTS CRAWL ACROSS THE SCREEN . . . HOLDING MY INDEX FINGER TO MY LIPS AND IMPLORING "SSHHHHHH!" THE IDEA OF THIS WAS TO HAVE A DIALOGUE WITH MY REVERED SLEEPING ALTER EGO . . . NOT TO CATAPULT HIM OUT OF HIS BED, AND HIS DREAMS OF THE STARS. PLEASE KEEP YOUR DOOR CLOSED. IF I FAIL IN SENDING YOU MY DAILY FILE . . . YOU CAN ALWAYS PRY IT FROM MY MACHINE IN THE MORNING.

ANYONE LIVING IN LOST ANGELES HAD BETTER NOT NEED ANY CONSTRUCTION WORK DONE FOR THE NEXT FEW MONTHS. EVERYBODY WHO HAS A HAMMER IS HERE . . . ON STAGES 15 AND 30 . . . BUILDING OUR SETS.

THE DODGERS LOST . . . TO PHILADELPHIA NO LESS. W. C. FIELDS MUST BE LAUGHING IN HIS GRAVE.

ONLY YOU COULD HAVE A FORMER AMBASSADOR FOR A SECRETARY.

ACC19 of 83 Oct 11

Also in the mail--tighten your seat belt--is a letter from Society Expeditions, which arranges little trips to the poles, China, the Galápagos, the Orient Express, etc., for up to $62,000 *per person*. Yes, you've guessed it: I quote: "Our goal is to charter the space shuttle for 40 to 60 dedicated flights beginning about 1992 . . . NASA has agreed to accept our proposal even though they cannot commit until Congress authorises . . . But we have offered the $100,000 of earnest money."

ACC20 of 83 Oct 12

Scott* is very interested in our correspondence, and I suggest you send him an edited/expurgated sample so he can get the flavour. (Do you have SpellStar? Sorry I asked . . .) I think it's already past 10,-000 words in less than a month. My God, people *will* be talking. . . .

---

* Scott Meredith. The best literary agent in the business, who sold this book.

PH21. OCTOBER 13, 1983

ON THE SUBJECT OF THE FIRST WEEK IN NOVEMBER. I AM
GOING TO ARECIBO ON THE SEVENTH OF NOVEMBER. IF
THERE ARE PEOPLE THERE WHO YOU WOULD LIKE ME TO
RELAY YOUR REGARDS TO . . . I WOULD BE HAPPY. (I AN-
TICIPATE A REPLY TOMORROW LIKE . . . GLAD YOU ARE
GOING TO ARECIBO . . . PLEASE SAY HELLO TO CLIVE AND
BETTY CONVEX . . . WE ALL BUILT THE DISH TOGETHER IN
'65.) DO YOU HAVE ANY IDEA OF THE HEADACHES YOU
HAVE CAUSED BY WRITING THAT WONDERFUL OPENING?
DO YOU? IT'S EASY TO TALK ABOUT PEOPLE WALKING LIKE
TINY SPECKS ON THE SURFACE OF THE BIG DISH. I HAVE TO
FIND A WAY TO GET THEM TO ACTUALLY DO IT . . . MUCH
LESS LUG ALL THAT GEAR UP THERE. WHEN THE GRIPS ARE
COMPLAINING ABOUT CARRYING PANAVISION CAMERAS
AND DOLLYS UP TO THE TOP OF THE DISH . . . I SHALL GIVE
THEM YOUR TELEPHONE NUMBER. I WOULDN'T WORRY IF I
WERE YOU . . . THEY PROBABLY WON'T BE ABLE TO GET
THROUGH TO COLOMBO . . . LIKE I COULDN'T ALL DAY
LONG.

ACC23 of 83 Oct 14

Since your dumb machine only accepted the file name of yesterday's
ACC22 and not the contents, here it
is again. Tear off at the dotted
line.
. . . .

Continuing ACC23

Arecibo will blow your mind. It was a
frustrating experience having just

one hour there in '73. Give my regards to Tom Clodfelter, who is now a programmer there but once built the Yellow Submarine that looked for the Loch Ness Monster.

What headache? If Carl* could do it in Cosmos #12, so can you. I've just run the tape again and it gives an excellent idea of the setup, but of course details will be completely different in "2010."

And there will be no problem, I hope, with the House of the Dolphins. In 1970 it was the home of T. A. P. Pryor of Sea Life Park, Honolulu, and Karen (who took me swimming with Li-Li, the first dolphin they could recall at will from the open sea). Anyway you might investigate.

Did you imagine I made these things up?

Talking of dolphins, please give my best to your neighbor Bob Radnitz, who optioned "Dolphin Island" aeons ago. He has some lovely artwork which he showed Steve and me on our visit to the studio and I am sure could be helpful. I do hope he can make that movie one day, though I no longer believe that dolphins are really intelligent. They are much too friendly to Man.

---

* Dr. Carl Sagan, whose magnificent television series "Cosmos" has been seen throughout the world.

PH22. OCTOBER 14, 1983

WE ARE HOT ON THE TRAIL OF THE DOLPHIN HOUSE. OF
COURSE I THOUGHT YOU MADE IT UP. YOU MEAN THERE
REALLY IS A MONOLITH WITH KEIR DULLEA OUT THERE?

WE HAVE HAD SANTA ANA WINDS HERE FOR THE PAST FEW
DAYS. THE SANTA ANAS ARE WINDS COMING FROM THE
DESERT . . . INSTEAD OF THE NORMAL DIRECTION, WHICH
IS FROM THE OCEAN. THE RESULT IS A HOT WIND . . .
EVEN AT NIGHT. MORE OFTEN THAN NOT THEY ARE THE
PERFECT CONDITIONS FOR FIRES HERE. THIS TIME WE
WERE SPARED. RAYMOND CHANDLER DESCRIBED THEM AS
THE TIMES WHEN HOUSEWIVES LOOK AT THEIR HUSBANDS'
THROATS DIFFERENTLY . . . WHILE THEY STAND IN THE
KITCHEN HOLDING A CARVING KNIFE. IT IS A STRANGE
WITCHING TIME HERE . . . WITH STRONG HOT BREEZES
RATTLING THE DRY BRANCHES OF TREES. IT IS A RESTLESS
TIME. I DO LOVE IT.

I SHALL CONVEY YOUR REGARDS TO TOM CLODFELTER.
WHAT HEADACHE? I'LL TELL YOU WHAT HEADACHE.
THERE IS A DIFFERENCE BETWEEN CARL SAGAN SHOOTING
SOME 16-MILLIMETER DOCUMENTARY FOOTAGE . . . AND
A FULL HOLLYWOOD FILM CREW USING THE EQUIPMENT WE
USE. I AM NOT COMPLAINING. I JUST WANT YOU TO FEEL
SORRY FOR ME.

MY FAMILY IS RUSSIAN. MY GRANDFATHER WAS AN EX-
TRAORDINARY MAN . . . WHO DID MORE TO BRING CUL-
TURE TO AMERICA THAN PROBABLY ANY INDIVIDUAL IN
HISTORY. HE ONLY HAD ONE CHILD . . . MY MOTHER . . .
AND I WAS HIS ONLY GRANDSON. WE WERE TERRIBLY
CLOSE. HE DIED A FEW YEARS AGO AT THE AGE OF
EIGHTY-SIX . . . AT WORK. I WEPT BECAUSE I KNEW HOW
MUCH I WOULD MISS HIM . . . HOWEVER, I ADMIRED THE

WAY HE DIED. ANY MAN WHO HAS BEEN LUCKY ENOUGH TO LIVE A PRODUCTIVE AND STIMULATING LIFE . . . WHO SAW THE ADVENT OF THE AUTOMOBILE . . . THE AIRPLANE . . . RADIO . . . TELEVISION . . . NUCLEAR ENERGY . . . THE COMPUTER . . . AND THE LANDING ON THE MOON . . . AND WHO ALSO MANAGED TO BECOME YOUR FRIEND IN THE PROCESS . . . THIS WAS A FORTUNATE MAN.

HAVE A RESTFUL WEEKEND. I SHALL MISS YOU. I WILL BE IN MY OFFICE TOMORROW (SATURDAY) FOR PART OF THE DAY. I WILL LEAVE THE MACHINE ON TONIGHT. I WILL TRY TO CONTACT YOUR MACHINE TOMORROW AFTERNOON . . . MY TIME. IF THERE IS NOTHING FOR ME . . . I WILL UNDERSTAND. I WILL ALSO NOT CLEAN YOUR DISK UP.

ACC24 of 83 Oct 15

Your grandfather sounds very much like Isaac Asimov's father. Immediately after his death Isaac wrote a very moving essay making the same point you do--one life spanning the first airplane and the first lunar landing.

By the way, even if we can't display messages while receiving, is it possible to print them out simultaneously? There's an Echo option I've not investigated. It's a damn nuisance waiting for Godot. . . . Sorry about that.

That's it for now. Have a good weekend. Will peek into your directory

your Monday night in case you have
been unable to send again.

PH23. OCTOBER 17, 1983

WHAT YEAR WAS TMA-1* FOUND ON THE MOON? I AM
GOING TO HAVE A BRIEF PROLOGUE AT THE BEGINNING OF
THE FILM (I THINK THE BEGINNING IS THE BEST PLACE FOR
A PROLOGUE) . . . AND I WANT TO DO IT CHRONOLOGI-
CALLY. I AM ASSUMING THAT THE DISCOVERY FLIGHT WAS
DURING THE YEAR 2001.

IT IS INTERESTING THAT STANLEY SAID THAT THE FILM
MIGHT HAVE TO BE CALLED 2002 BECAUSE OF LATE-
NESS. I HAD ONE OF THOSE WONDERFUL BUDGET MEET-
INGS LAST WEEK . . . WHERE I TOLD MGM I NEEDED X
DOLLARS TO DO SOMETHING. THEY RESPONDED THAT I
DIDN'T NEED ALL THAT. I SIMPLY TOLD THEM IF THEY
WANTED TO SAVE MONEY . . . WE SHOULD CALL THE FILM
2008. IF THEY WANTED 2010 . . . IT WAS GOING TO
COST THEM A LITTLE MORE. I THINK THEY UNDERSTOOD.

WORD ON THE DOLPHIN HOUSE. YOUR FRIEND . . . AS YOU
HAD STATED . . . NO LONGER OCCUPIES THE HOUSE. AS
OF NOW . . . NO ONE DOES. THE POOL IS NO LONGER SALT
WATER. WE ARE CHECKING ON THE CONDITION OF THE
HOUSE . . . AND IF IT IS AT ALL FEASIBLE TO USE IT. I
MIGHT WIND UP BUILDING SOMETHING IN FLORIDA . . . OR
PUERTO RICO . . . SINCE I WILL BE THERE FOR YOUR LIT-
TLE WHAT'S-THE-BIG-DEAL-SAGAN-DID-IT DISH.

I WANT YOU TO SEE "THE RIGHT STUFF." IN THE FIRST
PLACE I THINK IT IS WONDERFUL. SECONDLY . . . AS A

---

* Tycho Magnetic Anomaly-1, the black monolith found on the
moon in *2001: A Space Odyssey*.

JOURNALIST . . . I SPENT A LOT OF TIME COVERING THE
GEMINI AND APOLLO MISSIONS. I WOULD LOVE TO KNOW
WHAT YOU THINK OF IT.

ACC26 of 83 Oct 18

I was careful not to be too specific
about dates so you can do what you
like as long as it's self-consis-
tent. But I assumed that the discovery of TMA-1 was in 2001 and the
mission a couple of years later.

Sorry to learn that T.A.P.'s lovely
house is empty and wonder what happened to the beautiful marble floor.
But there's no need to go to Honolulu
except to study the layout, as
surely everything could be arranged
more easily down the coast at Sea
World.

PH24. OCTOBER 18, 1983

THE COMPANY OF PEOPLE WHO ARE NOW SPENDING THEIR
LIVES TRYING TO BRING YOUR BOOK TO THE SCREEN IS
MUSHROOMING. I NOW EMPLOY ABOUT ONE HUNDRED
FIFTY. IN TWO WEEKS ABOUT TEN MORE WILL BE ADDED. I
REMEMBER A LINE BY FRANÇOIS TRUFFAUT . . . "I
STARTED OUT TRYING TO MAKE THE GREATEST FILM IN THE
WORLD. I'M NOW HALFWAY THROUGH . . . AND ALL I WANT
TO DO IS GET THE THING FINISHED."

I HAVE BEEN ON THIS WORLDWIDE SEARCH . . . WITH NO
SUCCESS. I AM CALLING STANLEY TOMORROW, AND PER-
HAPS HE HAS THE ANSWER. WHAT EVER HAPPENED TO
DOUGLAS RAIN*? HE IS NOT LISTED IN BRITISH OR AMERI-
CAN EQUITY . . . SCREEN ACTORS' GUILD . . . NOWHERE.
WHEN DAVID BOWMAN PULLED OUT THOSE LITTLE PIECES
OF LUCITE . . . DID DOUGLAS RAIN VANISH? IF YOU KNOW
. . . PLEASE TELL ME.

WORD FROM HAWAII IS NOT GOOD. THE DOLPHIN HOUSE IS
NOT IN THE KIND OF SHAPE THAT MAKES ITS USE FEASIBLE.
I AM PROBABLY GOING TO HAVE TO BUILD SOMETHING.
THIS IS GOOD FOR THE CONSTRUCTION INDUSTRY . . . AND
NOT GOOD FOR MGM. NEXT TIME . . . WRITE ABOUT TWO
PEOPLE IN A LITTLE ROOM . . . NO END OF JUPITER . . .
NO FISH IN THE LVING ROOM . . . NO TELESCOPES BIGGER
THAN OHIO . . . OK? ALL RIGHT . . . THREE PEOPLE . . . A
BIG ROOM . . . I'LL THROW IN A COUCH. THAT'S MY FINAL
OFFER.

ACC27 of 83 Oct 19

I feel sad about Dolphin House (it
was a beautiful place), but as I suggested, San Diego would be a
slightly more convenient location.
If you want any high-level help at
Sea World call my friend and editor
Julian Muller at Harcourt Brace Jo-
vanovich. They own the joint.

I suggest you call the Toronto Star
re Rain. I never met him and the only

---

* The Canadian actor who was the voice of HAL in *2001*, and who
played the same role in the second film.

information I ever saw on him is in Agel's "The Making of 2001," which is still a good read. See especially p. 206. . . .

What's this about *fish* in the living room, for heaven's sake . . . That's a deadly insult in Delphinese (= *meshugana* approximately).

PH25. OCTOBER 19, 1983

I STARTED OUT WITH A BEAUTIFUL DISK. IT WAS SO CLEAN YOU COULD EAT OFF OF IT. NOW . . . EVERY DAY IT IS GET-TING MORE AND MORE CLUTTERED WITH PH'S AND ACC'S.

HAL IS ALIVE AND LIVING IN CANADA. WE FOUND DOUGLAS RAIN. I CALLED HIM . . . EXCEPT HE WAS OUT OF TOWN. I TOLD THE PERSON ON THE OTHER END OF THE TELEPHONE THAT CANADA WAS OUT OF TOWN . . . AND THAT ANY-PLACE MR. RAIN WENT WAS TOWARDS TOWN. I DON'T THINK HE UNDERSTOOD ME. AT ANY RATE . . . DOUGLAS RAIN IS SOMEWHERE IN CANADA UNAWARE OF THE FACT THAT HE HAS TO START TO PRACTICE SINGING "DAISY, DAISY."

I RECEIVED A LETTER FROM YOU LAST NIGHT. IT CON-TAINED THE LETTER FROM SATYAJIT RAY. I HELD IT UP TO A MIRROR. I PUT BLACK LIGHT ON IT. A FRIEND OF MINE IS A CRYPTOGRAPHER . . . SO I CALLED HIM OVER. NONE OF US COULD FIGURE IT OUT. HOWEVER . . . WE ALL AGREE THAT THE REASON WHY YOU UNDERSTOOD THE LETTER IS BECAUSE YOU HAVE THE SAME HANDWRITING. I SHALL KEEP IT . . . POSSIBLY FRAMED. I LOVE HIS WORK. I LOVE YOUR WORK. HERE IS HAVE ON ONE SHEET OF PAPER . . . A COMPLETELY UNDECIPHERABLE LETTER FROM HIM

. . . UNDERNEATH AN EQUALLY UNINTELLIGIBLE NOTE
FROM YOU. THIS WAS ACCOMPANIED BY A COPY OF SOME-
THING IN RUSSIAN. I ASSUME THAT THE INSCRIPTION IS IN
RUSSIAN. I HOPE THE INSCRIPTION IS IN RUSSIAN. I GET
THE FEELING I AM BEING GASLIT.

RE FISH IN THE LIVING ROOM. MY GRANDMOTHER TOOK ME
TO THE ZOO ONCE. I THINK IT WAS THE FIRST TIME SHE HAD
EVER SEEN AN ANIMAL OUTSIDE OF A BUTCHER SHOP. I
DRAGGED HER TO THE SEAL POND. SHE SAID SHE DIDN'T
LIKE FISH. I TOLD HER THEY WEREN'T FISH. SHE SAID IF
THEY SWIM . . . THEY'RE FISH. I SAID, "GRANDMA . . . I
SWIM." SHE SAID, "NOT LIKE A FISH." THERE IS A CER-
TAIN KIND OF LOGIC YOU CAN'T ARGUE WITH.

I AM LOOKING IN THE FLORIDA AREA BECAUSE IT IS MUCH
MORE LOGICAL TO GO FROM PUERTO RICO TO FLORIDA
. . . THAN FROM PUERTO RICO TO SAN DIEGO. I WILL KNOW
IF I HAVE A CHANCE OF FINDING IT IN THE NEXT WEEK OR
TWO.

I READ THE CRITIQUE OF YOUR WORK YOU SENT ME. IT AL-
WAYS ASTOUNDS ME HOW PEOPLE WHO DON'T DO ANY-
THING . . . SPEND SO MUCH OF THEIR TIME TRYING TO
FIND FAULT WITH WHAT SOMEONE ELSE HAS DONE. THE
SMALL MATTER THAT HE WAS WRONG IS IRRELEVANT. I
MYSELF TRY TO NEVER LET FACTS GET IN MY WAY. IT IS
MORE THIS STRANGE DYNAMIC THAT HAS BEEN IN MOTION
IN THE ARTS FOR SO LONG. I DON'T UNDERSTAND THE REL-
ISH THAT THESE NEWTS HAVE IN LOOKING FOR TINY EPI-
DERMAL BLEMISHES IN THE SKIN OF SOMETHING
WONDERFUL . . . OR MORE TO THE POINT . . . SOME-
THING THAT THEY DIDN'T DO. I WONDER HOW MANY OF
THESE PEOPLE COULD STAND THE SAME SCRUTINY THEY
APPLY TO OTHERS.

PH25. PAGE 2:

I OFTEN FIND LAVISH PRAISE MUCH MORE FOOLISH THAN
CRITICISM. (THAT PROBABLY HAS SOMETHING WITH BEING

JEWISH.) I REMEMBER WHEN I WAS IN LONDON . . . FILM-
ING "OUTLAND." A VERY IMPORTANT CRITIC FOR A VERY
IMPORTANT AND HALLOWED PUBLICATION WANTED TO
COME TO PINEWOOD TO HAVE LUNCH WITH ME. I SAID
SURE. HE WAS ALMOST REVERENTIAL WHEN WE MET . . .
WHICH IS ENOUGH TO GET ME VERY SUSPICIOUS. HE SAID
THAT "CAPRICORN ONE" HAD FIRMLY ESTABLISHED ME
AS ONE OF THE YOUNG MASTERS OF AMERICAN CINEMA. I
TOLD HIM THANK YOU . . . AND THEN I HAD TO DRINK A LOT
OF WATER. HE WENT ON TO SAY THAT THE ASPECT OF THE
FILM THAT PROVED TO HIM I HAD ACHIEVED THIS LEVEL
. . . THAT I HAD ARRIVED AT THE SUMMIT . . . WAS MY KU-
BRICK HOMAGE IN THE FILM. I MUST SAY THAT ANYONE
WITH EVEN A SHRED OF CHARACTER WOULD HAVE
STOPPED THE WHOLE THING RIGHT THEN AND THERE. NOT
BEING BURDENED WITH CHARACTER . . . I SPENT THE
REST OF THE LUNCH TRYING TO FIND OUT WHAT THE HELL
HE WAS TALKING ABOUT . . . WITHOUT HIM KNOWING I
HADN'T A CLUE. BY THE SECOND COFFEE . . . HE RE-
VEALED IT. IN THE END OF THE FILM . . . THERE IS A SCENE
WHERE A MAN WHO HAS BEEN RUNNING ACROSS THE DES-
ERT BREAKS INTO AN EMPTY GAS STATION. HE HAS TO
MAKE A TELEPHONE CALL. THERE IS NO CHANGE IN THE
TELEPHONE. HE ISN'T CARRYING ANY MONEY ON HIM. SO
. . . HE TAKES A CROWBAR . . . AND PRIES OPEN A COCA-
COLA MACHINE. WELL . . . AS ANY FOOL CAN SEE . . .
THAT IS, OF COURSE, A TRIBUTE TO "DR. STRANGE-
LOVE." I DIDN'T TELL HIM THAT HE WAS CRAZIER THAN
STRANGELOVE HIMSELF. I THINK I SAID SOMETHING SLIMY
LIKE "OH . . . YOU CAUGHT IT."

I BRING THIS BORING STORY UP . . . ONLY BECAUSE ONCE
I REALIZED HOW UNDESERVED SO MUCH OF THE CRITICAL
PRAISE IS . . . I BEGAN TO REALIZE THAT AN EQUAL
AMOUNT OF THE NASTY REVIEWS ARE JUST AS SILLY. WE
ARE CERTAINLY NOT AS GOOD AS SOME PEOPLE SAY.
HOWEVER . . . THE GOOD PART IS THAT WE MAY NOT BE
AS BAD AS THE OTHERS SAY.

ACC28 of 20 1983 Oct 20

The Government has just announced that the local Earth Satellite station is saturated and the country will have to plug into a new submarine cable. It's all our fault.

I'm sure Sea World Orlando will be happy to co-operate. Also delighted you've found Douglas Rain. I hope he doesn't worry about being typed.

Let me know if you really can't read Satyajit's fine Indian hand and I'll send a translation. I assume you have some Russian experts around and you must admit that Alexei writes elegant Cyrillic. So did Yuri Gagarin--I am very proud of a personal inscription I have from him.

I hope you've passed on to Judy-Lynn del Rey* (She Who Must Be Obeyed) my amazing foresight in mentioning this week's Nobelist in physics on page 275.

Wish you could have seen me this morning in my purple Chancellor's robes when President Jayawardene made me the first Honorable Fellow of our Institution of Engineers--an award for a misspent youth devoted to playing with Meccano all the time I wasn't reading s.f.

---

* The publisher of Del Rey Books.

PH26. OCTOBER 20, 1983

ANOTHER IN THE CATALOGUE OF DIFFERENCES BETWEEN
THE TWO OF US. YOU LEFT YOUR LITTLE KEYBOARD . . .
DONNED PURPLE ROBES . . . AND MET WITH THE PRESI-
DENT. I TURNED OFF THE LIGHTS . . . NOTICED THAT I HAD
A BUTTON MISSING ON MY ALREADY FRAYED SHIRT . . .
AND MET WITH TWO ELECTRICIANS, WHO TOLD ME THEY
HAD LOOKED AT MY LIGHTING SKETCHES AND THAT I WAS
CRAZY.

I SPOKE WITH DOUGLAS RAIN TODAY. HE SAID HE IS A BIG
FAN OF YOURS. HE DOES SOUND LIKE HAL.

YOU ASKED ME TO LET YOU KNOW IF I CAN'T READ MR.
RAY'S FINE INDIAN HAND. I CAN'T READ MR. RAY'S FINE IN-
DIAN HAND.

I ALSO CAN'T READ YOUR FINE BRITISH HAND.

I ALSO CAN'T READ ALEXEI'S FINE SOVIET HAND.

I DON'T KNOW IF YOU HAVE HEARD OR NOT. LAST NIGHT
. . . THERE WERE REPORTS ON TELEVISION THAT TWO SO-
VIET COSMONAUTS ARE TRAPPED IN SPACE. THE VEHICLE
THAT WAS SUPPOSED TO GO UP AND GET THEM BLEW UP
SOME WEEKS AGO. OUR SHUTTLE IS IN SOME TROUBLE.
THERE IS A PROBLEM WITH THE LINING OF THE FUEL
TANKS. SO FAR . . . THE RUSSIAN GOVERNMENT IS STAT-
ING PUBLICLY THAT THERE IS NO PROBLEM . . . AND THEY
HAVE NO NEED OF OUR ASSISTANCE. WE ARE ALSO TAKING
THIS OPPORTUNITY TO NOT OFFER ANY ASSISTANCE.
EVERY DAY THAT PASSES FILLS ME WITH ASTONISHMENT
AS TO HOW PROPHETIC OUR FILM IS. I TRULY WISH IT
WASN'T.

PH27. OCTOBER 21, 1983

I AM SORRY IF YOU TRIED TO CONTACT ME AND FOUND NO
ANSWER. I WAS OUT OF THE OFFICE ALL AFTERNOON.
MOST OF THIS DAY WAS SPENT IN THE MODEL SHOP. I AM
FORTUNATE TO HAVE THE FINEST CRAFTSMEN IN THE
WORLD BUILDING THESE MODELS.

I HOPE YOUR FRIEND JAMES OBERG IS CORRECT. ALL OF
THE REPORTS ON AMERICAN TELEVISION DO NOT AGREE
WITH HIM. THEY ALL SAY THAT THE VEHICLE IS DRIFTING
BADLY . . . AND THAT THERE IS THE POSSIBILITY THAT
THERE IS A PRESSURE LEAK.

ACC30 of 83 Oct 22

Jim Oberg may be a useful contact; he
knows more about the Russian space
programme than anyone outside the
CIA (and possibly inside). And unlike them he's able--nay, willing
--to talk. Did I mention that my am-
bassador-secretary built the 2001
space station? He started life as an
engineer-architect and was Director of Ceylon's Public Works Dept in
the early sixties, before a change
of government made him decide to go
to the UK, and I got him a job with
Stanley. He may be able to give some
advice on the models, though I doubt

it, as by this time the art must have
progressed enormously.

Here's something that may make your
flesh creep. When I tried to save
this file, for the first time I got
the message FATAL ERROR--DIRECTORY FULL.

I'm meeting Thomas Mann's daughter
on Tuesday.

PH28. OCTOBER 22, 1983

THIS WAS A GOOD SATURDAY. MOVIE STUDIOS ON SATUR-
DAYS ARE LIKE THEATERS AND ATHLETIC STADIUMS THE
DAY BEORE A PERFORMANCE OR A GAME. THERE IS THIS
CAVERNOUS FACILITY . . . THAT IS ALWAYS FILLED WITH
ENORMOUS ENERGY AND CACOPHONY . . . AND IT IS
EMPTY AND SILENT. AT MGM . . . YOU FEEL THE GHOSTS. I
LOVE IT. I ACTUALLY GOT SOME WRITING DONE. AT THIS
STAGE . . . I AM WILLING TO SETTLE FOR QUANTITY . . .
AS I GAVE UP ON QUALITY A LONG TIME AGO.

TELL THOMAS MANN'S DAUGHTER THAT HER FATHER
CAUSED ME NO LITTLE GRIEF IN COLLEGE ENGLISH.

ACC31 of 83 Oct 24

The BBC has just announced that sup-
plies have now reached the Soviet
space station, and quotes NASA as

saying that it would be willing to
offer the Shuttle as a rescue craft
but that "the Russians would rather
die." Just like the Chinese in 2010.
History is breathing down our neck.
I hope we don't get pickets round the
theaters because our Russians are
nice guys.

This morning's paper says that
Spielberg* is coming here on a holi-
day. I don't believe it--but please
check.

Now off to "Clash of the Titans"--
not very good and I've seen it before, but I'm a sucker for this kind
of nonsense.

PH29. OCTOBER 24, 1983

I DON'T HAVE TO WORRY ABOUT MY DISK GETTING OVER-
LOADED. YOU WILL YELL AT ME ABOUT THE MESSY DI-
RECTORY LONG BEFORE THAT.

THIS IS A TERRIBLE DAY. THE HEADLINES ABOUT DEAD
AMERICAN SOLDIERS . . . THE TELEVISION INTERVIEWS
WITH BELLICOSE SENATORS AND WHITE HOUSE SPOKES-
MEN . . . AND THE COLLAGE OF PARENTS, WHO ARE TRY-
ING TO MAKE SOME SENSE OUT OF THEIR CHILDREN BEING
CRUSHED IN THE RUBBLE OF A LEBANESE AIRPORT BUILD-
ING . . . I HAVE SEEN THEM ALL BEFORE . . . WHEN I WAS

---

* Steven Spielberg, promising young American movie director who
has made some little-known films such as *E.T.*, *Close Encounters of
the Third Kind*, *Jaws*, *Raiders of the Lost Ark*, etc. You may catch
them at your local art theater.

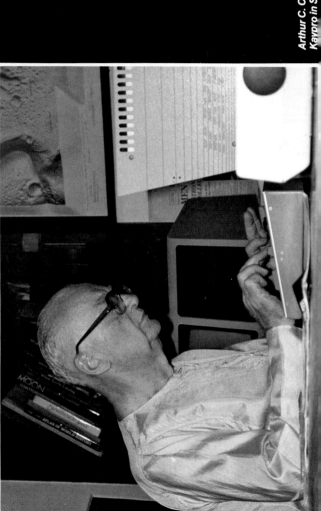

Arthur C. Clarke at his Kaypro in Sri Lanka.

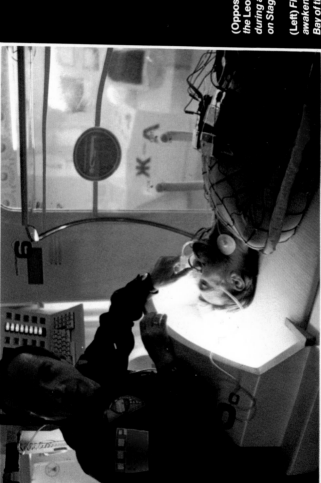

(Opposite) The bridge of the Leonov is flipped during an action sequence on Stage 15 at MGM.

(Left) Floyd (Scheider) is awakened in the Medical Bay of the Leonov.

Arthur C. Clarke and his assistant Steven Jongeward with the famous "fish."

Floyd (Scheider) prepares for the mission while the dolphins try to distract him.

The Very Large Array Radio Telescope, which substituted for Arecibo in the film's opening

Floyd (Scheider) tells Milson (McEachin) why they must go on the mission. Note Arthur C. Clarke feeding the birds as he makes a cameo appearance in the film.

(Opposite) The Probe
is operated by
Orlov (Rudnik) as
Brailovsky (Baskin)
looks on intently.

Dr. Chandra
(Bob Balaban)
reactivates HAL

Dave Bowman
(Keir Dullea) delivers
the final message to
Floyd as he gazes at
his old friend HAL

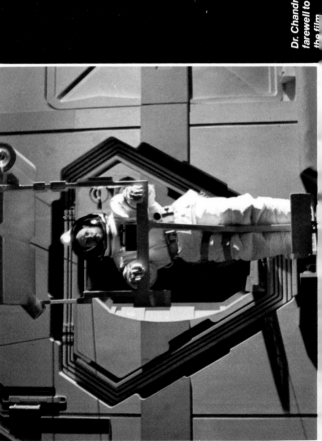

Dr. Chandra (Bob Balaban) says farewell to HAL in the final sequence of the film.

(Right) Floyd (Scheider) demonstrates escape plan using a writing pen, as it floats in the zero-G atmosphere of the Leonov bridge.

(Opposite) The Russian Crew in the Pod Bay of the Leonov.

(Opposite) Floyd (Scheider) greets Curnow (Lithgow) and Dr. Chandra (Balaban) as they awaken from deep hibernation sleep in the Leonov Medical Bay.

(Left) Curnow (Lithgow) struggles toward the spinning Discovery, the first EVA activity in 2010.

Peter Hyams at his Kaypro in the 2010 office at MGM.

IN MY TWENTIES. I HATE THOSE PICTURES. THE LAST THING YOUNG BOYS SHOULD SEE . . . IS NOT THE HORROR THAT THESE YOUNG BOYS SAW. AS I SAID BEFORE . . . THIS FILM IS BECOMING MORE AND MORE PROPHETIC . . . AND I SO DEARLY WISH IT WASN'T.

THE MORE I READ THIS BOOK . . . THE MORE I AM TOUCHED BY WHAT A KIND AND WONDERFUL MAN YOU ARE. I WISH YOUR PACIFISM AND YOUR POETIC SENSE OF WONDER ABOUT THE FUTURE . . . TURNS OUT TO BE AS ACCURATE AS YOUR ASTONISHING ABILITY TO PREDICT OUR SCIENTIFIC PROGRESS.

ACC32 of 83 Oct 25

After I'd addressed the Pacem in Maribus conference* this morning, I told Elizabeth Mann Borgese that her father had caused you problems.

PH30. OCTOBER 25, 1983

I SPENT MUCH OF THE DAY WITH JPL . . . AND SPECIFI-CALLY DR. TERRILE.† WE HAVE BEEN GOING THROUGH A

---

* The series of conferences known as Pacem in Maribus is devoted to the peaceful uses of the world's oceans for navigation, fishing, and such later developments as deep-ocean mining.
† Dr. Richard J. Terrile, planetary scientist with the Optical and In-frared Astronomy Group, Earth and Space Sciences Division of the Jet Propulsion Laboratory. He has been monitoring the scientific content of the movie, but don't blame him for everything that happens.

LOT OF DIALOGUE ABOUT THE AEROBRAKING SEQUENCE. I
HAVE BEEN READING A GREAT DEAL OF DATA RECENTLY
ABOUT THIS IDEA. TERRILE AND HIS COLLEAGUES HAVE
COME UP WITH AN INTERESTING SUGGESTION. I WOULD
LIKE YOUR THOUGHTS.

THEIR POINT IS THAT THE WHOLE IDEA OF A HEAT SHIELD
DOES NOT MAKE A LOT OF SENSE . . . FROM A PAYLOAD
STANDPOINT. (YOU EVEN MAKE REFERENCE TO THIS IN
THE BOOK.) THEY SAY THAT THE NEWEST THEORIES CEN-
TER AROUND THE IDEA OF TURNING THE SPACECRAFT
AROUND SO THAT THE ENGINES ARE THE LEADING EDGE.
BY FIRING THE ENGINES . . . AN ENVELOPE IS CREATED
AROUND THE SPACECRAFT. THE DENSER THE ATMO-
SPHERE . . . THE CLOSER THE ENVELOPE GETS TO THE
PERIMETER OF THE CRAFT. THIS CREATES . . . AMONG
OTHER THINGS . . . A RATHER DAZZLING PYROTECHNICAL
DISPLAY . . . AS THE EFFECT OF THE ENGINE THRUST IS
FOLDED BACK ALONG THE SPACECRAFT. THEY FIRMLY BE-
LIEVE THAT THIS ALLOWS A CRAFT OF ALMOST ANY DESIGN
TO AEROBRAKE . . . ALMOST EXACTLY AS YOU WROTE
THE SEQUENCE.

MY ONLY REACTIONS ARE THAT IT SEEMS FACINATING. I
HAVE NEVER SEEN ANYTHING LIKE THIS BEFORE. IF IT IS
THE MOST FEASIBLE WAY TO AEROBRAKE . . . THEN I AM
MORE INTERESTED . . . EVEN IF IT MEANS THAT OUR
HEROES ARE FORGING TOWARDS THE FUTURE RECTUM
FIRST.

ACC33 of 83 Oct 26

I too am fascinated by the idea of
turning Leonov into a flying fart. I
would never have dared suggest such

a crazy idea but if JPL says it will work that's splendid, especially if it will be much more dramatic. However, it may take some explaining, as a naive viewer (i.e., 90% of the audience) will think it's pure rocket braking . . . so what. . . .

I must say it's a bit scary. Nothing (much) can go wrong with a passive heat shield, but a dynamic system would be really tough on the nerves. Any of a dozen things could malfunction and lead to Instant Barbecued Astronauts. Which is splendid scriptwise.

I've just had a cable from Moscow saying that part one* is about to appear and it's quote absolutely necessary to get from you as soon as possible a short appeal to the Soviet readers. Hope to receive kind words of peace and understanding between people, as in fact the novel is devoted to them unquote. I'm brooding over this.

ACC34 of 83 Oct 27

Couldn't get through this morning to check your directory. Were you switched on?

---

* Of *2010: Odyssey Two*.

Nothing new from this end--just
leaving for Pacem in Maribus farewell reception being thrown by the
Minister of Foreign Affairs. You
should see me in national dress,
looking exactly like the late Dr No
(except for the claws).

Will remain on ANS and will try to
peek at your disk when I get back
around 1600 GMT.

ACC35 of 83 Oct 28

Last night dined next to Jacques Pi-
card, who (with Don Walsh) took
Trieste down to 37,000 feet in the
Marianas (one of the few records
that will never be beaten unless
anyone finds a deeper hole). He's
seen "2001" several times and thinks
it's the most beautiful movie ever.
Wants to know how you can top it.
Good question. . . .

What a day; a blizzard of cables and
phone calls. The opening of the
Clarke Centre* now set for 30 November with live TV from Director-Gen-
eral of UNESCO. And now the Japanese

---

* Established by my friends in Sri Lanka adjacent to the University
of Moratuwa some 12 miles south of Colombo, Sri Lanka, the Clarke
Centre's purpose will be to train personnel in the fields of communications, computers, energy, and robotics, particularly as they apply
to third world countries.

want to give it a quite large (20 inches or more) *optical* telescope, which is another challenge. When shall I ever get back to the novel . . . It was abandoned months ago at 20,000 words . . .

I don't think I should be talking to you, since we're technically at war. Isn't Grenada part of the Commonwealth?

PH32. OCTOBER 28, 1983

THERE IS MORE ON THE AEROBRAKING. I HAVE SPOKEN WITH SOME PEOPLE AT BOEING AEROSPACE. THEY ARE WORKING ON A COMBINATION OF DR. TERRILE'S CONCEPT AND A THING CALLED A BALLUTE. A BALLUTE IS A GIANT GAS-FILLED BALLOON . . . IN THE SHAPE OF A ROUNDED APOLLO CAPSULE . . . THAT FITS OVER THE LEADING EDGE OF THE SPACECRAFT. THIS THING IS TRULY ENORMOUS . . . AT LEAST HALF THE SIZE OF THE SPACECRAFT. IT IS HOLLOW AT THE LEADING (FLAT) EDGE. THE NOW INFAMOUS LEONOV SPHINCTER CAN DELIVER ITS RECTAL PLASMA. THE ADVANTAGE OF THIS METHOD IS THAT THE BALLUTE SLOWS THE CRAFT DOWN WHILE THE ENGINE THRUST HELPS CREATE A HYPERSONIC SHOCK WAVE. THE RESULT IS MUCH LESS FUEL EXPENDED. AGAIN . . . I AM NOT SURE WHICH IS BETTER FOR THE FILM. THE FIRST WAY . . . ENGINES ONLY . . . IS MUCH MORE PYROTECHNICAL. THE SECOND WAY . . . THE GREAT BALLUTE . . . IS FUEL EFFICIENT. WHAT DO YOU THINK? YOUR OPINION IS VITAL TO ME. ONE . . . BECAUSE THE AUTHOR'S INTENT IS MY PRIME OBJECTIVE. TWO . . . BECAUSE IF IT LOOKS STUPID . . . I CAN BLAME YOU.

ACC36 of 83 Oct 31

I don't feel very strongly about
either aerobraking system but feel
that as you are making a movie and
not actually going to Jupiter (yet,
anyway) you should not let the engineers brainwash you with talk of ef-
ficiency. As long as the method
chosen is plausible, the decision
should be based on such factors as
visual impact, audience comprehen-
sion, plot requirements, and spe-
cial-effects cost/feasibility. I
have a hunch that the ballute would
look silly, but I may be wrong.

We went through a similar process of
agonising reappraisal on "2001,"
when the Orion (nuclear pulse)
project was declassified. The art
department made design studies but
Stanley finally dropped the idea
because (a) no one would believe it,
even if it did make technical sense;
(b) after Strangelove, who wanted
more bombs?

I've just recalled that one detail
now dating "2001" is the Bell System
logo . . . Maybe Stanley should re-
shoot that sequence. (The little
girl* has now made her first movie,

---

* At the beginning of *2001*, there is a scene in which Heywood Floyd
makes a call to Earth and is answered by his little daughter, played in
the movie by Stanley Kubrick's own daughter, Vivienne. She is now
a very good filmmaker in her own right.

shown on British TV, of Daddy making
"The Shining." He bought her a camera, not a bush-baby.)

added Oct 31

Tried to send this on the 29th but
couldn't connect. Do you mean you
weren't working on Saturday? Shame
on you . . . Still, I had one of my
rare Sundays off, going to buffet
lunch in a new hotel 40 km up the
coast. Claims to have the biggest
swimming pool in the world, but I
don't believe it. We could easily
see the other side.

It's been a busy day. In the morning
I had to give the keynote address in
our largest hall to an international
group of conference organisers--
subject, the impact of technology on
their business. Discussed telecon-
ferencing and mentioned our dialogues.

Now I've just come from an hour-long
meeting with the President, the
Prime Minister and the Minister of
Foreign Affairs. His Excellency has
asked me to draft a speech he's giving next week, declaring war on the
United States.

Well . . . actually it's to open a
conference on remote sensing, and
I'll lend him Charles Sheffield's
beautiful "Earthwatch" so he can see
what it's all about.

PH31. OCTOBER 31, 1983

THE EXTERIOR OF HALF OF THE DISCOVERY COMMAND MODULE BALL IS ALMOST COMPLETE. LEONOV LOOKS LIKE A JIGSAW PUZZLE. THIS GIANT SOUND STAGE LOOKS LIKE A HUGE WOODEN BALL CAME CRASHING THROUGH AND FELL ON SOMEBODY'S SETS.

A FURTHER UPDATE ON THE AEROBRAKING. I HAVE DOUBLE CONFIRMATION ON THIS THEORY. ANOTHER INTERESTING FACET IS THAT AEROBRAKING WILL PRODUCE A CONTRAIL OF OVER TWO HUNDRED MILES. WE MAY ACTUALLY HAVE A DECENT-LOOKING FILM.

NEW DESIGNS ON THE LEONOV NOSE COME IN TOMORROW. SINCE I AM NOT GOING TO USE A HEAT SHIELD . . . THE BOW HAD TO BE CHANGED. THE LEONOV'S ANUS WILL BE THE NEW STAR. ''2010'' SHOULD BE A GIANT SUCCESS AT PROCTOLOGY CONVENTIONS.

PH33. OCTOBER 31, 1983

THERE IS NOT A LOT TO REPORT. I AM MEETING WITH SYD MEAD AND DR. TERRILE TOMORROW . . . AND WILL MAKE A FINAL DETERMINATION ON THE AEROBRAKING. IT WILL DEPEND ON WHICH DESIGNS LOOK THE BEST.

TONIGHT IS HALLOWEEN. THOUSANDS OF MUNCHKINS AND THINGS THAT GO BUMP IN THE NIGHT CAREEN FROM HOUSE TO HOUSE . . . ASKING FOR CANDY AND CAUSING WHATEVER HAVOC THEY CAN GET AWAY WITH.

I MADE A BRIEF ANNOUNCEMENT TRAILER FOR THE THEATERS . . . WHICH IS A BIT UNUSUAL THIS FAR IN ADVANCE.

IT SIMPLY SAID THAT IN 1984 THEY WILL SEE 2010 . . .
26 YEARS AHEAD OF ITS TIME. I RAN THE TRAILER SATUR-
DAY NIGHT AT A PACKED THEATER HERE. THE REACTION
WAS SO STUNNING . . . I AM BEGINNING TO BELIEVE THAT
WE MAY JUST HAVE SOMETHING HERE.

ACC37 of 83 Nov 1

You don't say what the audience did
--climb up the screen like the
zonked-out '68ers?

Look forward to results of your
aerobraking conference. Incidentally Asoka* is the big comet expert
and could be useful. Gehrels† is the
authority on asteroids at the Lunar
and Planetary Lab, University of
Arizona.

PH34. NOVEMBER 1, 1983

LIKE WATER DRIPPING FROM A LEAKY FAUCET . . . I FIND
MYSELF ALREADY GROWING DAMP WITH NOVEMBER . . .
AND A START DATE IN FEBRUARY. I HAVE ENOUGH COLD
SWEAT TO FLOOD THE PLACE.

THE AEROBRAKING . . . TA DA. I HAVE DECIDED TO USE A
COMBINATION OF BOTH SYSTEMS. ONE . . . BECAUSE IT

---

* Dr. Asoka Mendis
† Dr. Tom Gehrels

WILL LOOK GOOD . . . AND TWO . . . BECAUSE IF I USE
ONLY THE ENGINES . . . IT IS NOT REALLY AEROBRAKING
ACCORDING TO JPL. SINCE YOUR WHOLE CONCEPT IS
AEROBRAKING . . . I FEEL IT IS IMPORTANT TO TRY TO DO
IT. I WORKED WITH SYD AND DR. TERRILE . . . AND DE-
SIGNED A SERIES OF BALLUTES THAT INFLATE BEHIND
THE ENGINE CLUSTER. THE ENGINES WILL BE IN WHAT
THEY CALL ENGINE IDLE DURING THE AEROBRAKING. THAT
IS, THEY WILL HARDLY USE ANY FUEL . . . HOWEVER,
THEY WILL PROVIDE A CUSHION FOR THE ENGINE CLUSTER
ITSELF. THE BALLUTE WILL PROTECT THE LEONOV. THE
WHOLE BUSINESS IS QUITE FIERY . . . WITH A 200-MILE
CONTRAIL . . . A SHOWER OF GLOWING PLASMA . . . AND
IT COULD POSSIBLY SCARE THE PISS OUT OF THE AUDI-
ENCE. IT ALSO IS THE CORRECT WAY . . . WHICH IS A
RATHER CONVENIENT BONUS. SO . . . AFTER ALL THIS
TIME AND STUDY . . . AFTER OUR COLLABORATION . . .
AFTER THE CONSULTATION WITH BOEING AND JPL . . . WE
HAVE ARRIVED AT THE RECTAL-FIRST-BIG-BALLUTE-
PLASMA-SHOWER-GAS-SAVING-LOW-ENERGY-FART-
AEROBRAKING MANEUVER AS CONCIEVED BY ARTHUR C.
CLARKE. (IT CAN ALSO BE REFERRED TO AS THE OLD
R.F.B.B.P.S.G.S.L.E.F.A.M. PLOY.)

ACC38 of Nov 2

Did I ever tell you what Steve did to
Buzz Aldrin* when he wanted him to
meet me at the Bel Air? After spending ten minutes telling him how to
reach the place (not, I should have

---

* Aldrin landed on the Moon with Neil Armstrong, in the historic
Apollo 11 first mission.

thought, one of the more inconspicuous local landmarks), he finally
exclaimed in exasperation: "Colo-
nel Aldrin, you found your way to the
Moon. Surely you can find the Bel Air
Hotel."

PH35. NOVEMBER 2, 1983

THERE IS SOME FETAL YET ENCOURAGING PROGRESS
FROM JOHN WHITNEY AND THE JUPITER IMAGE. IO IS AN-
OTHER CHALLENGE, ALTHOUGH I HAVE LUCKED OUT IN DR.
TERRILE. HE IS THE MAN WHO WAS RESPONSIBLE FOR
GATHERING AND INTERPRETING ALL OF THE VOYAGER
DATA. AS A RESULT . . . WE HAVE ACCESS TO IMAGES AND
INFORMATION FROM IO AND EUROPA THAT NO ONE HAS
EVER SEEN.

ACC39 of 83 Nov 3

Nearly had a heart attack last night
when I found the Kaypro dead in the
water. The 1 amp fuse at the back had
blown, presumably through a voltage
surge. I assume that my power backup
does not contain a voltage stabil-
iser and must look into this. I advise you to instal one if you
haven't.

PH36. NOVEMBER 3, 1983

YES . . . I HAVE A SURGE PROTECTOR . . . ON ALL THREE
COMPUTERS HERE. I LEARNED OF ITS IMPORTANCE THE
HARD WAY . . . WHEN MY WORD PROCESSOR THREW AN
EMBOLISM AND DESTROYED FORTY PAGES OF A SCRIPT
TWO YEARS AGO. I'M SO PARANOID . . . I AM THINKING
ABOUT GETTING SURGE PROTECTORS FOR THE SURGE
PROTECTOR.

I RECIEVED SYD'S BALLUTE DRAWINGS. THEY ARE EXCEL-
LENT.

I AM LEAVING FOR ARECIBO TOMORROW. I WILL GO TO NEW
YORK OVER THE WEEKEND . . . AND RETURN HERE TUES-
DAY. SINCE THERE IS NO ONE ELSE HERE CRAZY ENOUGH
TO TRY TO WORK THIS THING . . . I WILL SHUT IT OFF
AFTER I SEND THIS MESSAGE. SO YOU WON'T HAVE ME TO
YELL AT FOR THE NEXT FOUR DAYS. IF YOU FIND THE VOID
TOO GREAT . . . YELL AT ME ANYWAY . . . I'LL PROBABLY
HEAR YOU.

ACC40 of 83 Nov 8

Hope you had a nice trip to Arecibo
and look forward to your reactions.
I'm sure the studio will be delighted if you decide it's cheaper
to build the whole thing in the back
lot.

Back to PH36. I've no sympathy for
anyone who loses forty pages because
he forgot to SAVE regularly. Most
I've ever lost is one page . . .
well, maybe two . . . or just possibly three . . .

London Daily Telegraph, 4 November
decides that "Star Chamber"* "might
have had some appeal to the intel-
lect . . . in the legal technicali-
ties, and also in the moral
questions posed, but these aspects
are submerged in the over-enthusi-
astic illustration of crimes remarkable for sadism and violence.
The acting is also over-emphatic."
The first criticism certainly won't
apply to ''2010''; we'll have to see
about the second. (Who are you getting? Hal Holbrook would be a good
Floyd. But then he can be a good anyone. Were you tempted to offer Dr
Chandra to Ben Kingsley?!†) I'll be
meeting the other Dr Chandra (see
Chapter 52) here next month. I hope
he doesn't think . . .

saving at this point, like all intelligent WordStarrers. . . .

Some trivia that have accumulated
over the w.e.:

Popular Science for October has
pictures of NASA's re-entry designs
for Titan, etc. Sounds interesting.

The paperback "2010" came out in
the UK two weeks ago and instantly jumped to #1. The adverts
say: "Don't wait for the movie."

---

* Peter Hyams' last movie before *2010: Odyssey Two*, which was released during the writing of the screenplay.
† The actor who leaped to fame with his Oscar-winning performance
as Gandhi.

Obviously   a   lot   of   people
aren't. . . .

The local papers have a nice quote
from a recent visitor: "Sri Lanka is
a movie set built by God"--G. Lucas.

Just got back from a fascinating
breakfast with Ambassador-at-Large
Vernon Walters, retired Deputy-
Director of the CIA. He tells me that
Clare Booth Luce (who he brought to
see me on my last visit to Washington) has now sold ''The House of the
Dolphins.'' (When I wrote "2010," I
had no idea that there really was a
place with this name! I don't know
what T.A.P. called his house.)

I told General Walters that you
might let him see the set if he knew
how to keep a secret.

PH37. NOVEMBER 8, 1983

I SPENT MOST OF THE LAST FOUR DAYS IN AIRPLANES. I
DON'T KNOW IF I WILL BE ABLE TO EAT WITH REGULAR-
SIZED FORKS FOR A WHILE.

ARECIBO IS, OF COURSE, ONE OF THE WONDERS OF THE
WORLD. IT IS ALSO, HOWEVER, SOMETHING OF A DISAP-
POINTMENT. IT IS FILTHY. I MEAN TRULY FILTHY. IT LOOKS
LIKE AN ABANDONED PARKING LOT. THEY SAY THEY CAN'T
POSSIBLY CLEAN IT. WE'RE TALKING REALLY DIRTY. I HAD
THE STRANGEST FEELING . . . THAT MIGHT NOT BE UN-
DERSTANDABLE OR TRANSLATABLE. I HAD THE FEELING
THAT IF I BEGAN 2010 THERE . . . IT WOULD LOOK LIKE A

LOCATION THAT WAS NO LONGER IN USE. I DON'T KNOW. I
HAVE TO SPEND A FEW DAYS DRAWING. I FIND I LEARN
MORE FROM DRAWING A SCENE THAN BY TALKING ABOUT
IT. ONE OF THE ALTERNATIVES IS THE VLA* IN NEW MEX-
ICO. I AM SURE YOU KNOW ABOUT IT. I SAW SOME PHOTO-
GRAPHS . . . AND I MAY GO DOWN THIS WEEKEND TO TAKE
A LOOK. IT COULD BE WONDERFUL . . . OR IT COULD BE,
AS MY MOTHER SAYS, DREK.

HOW DO I CHECK TO SEE THE REMAINING SPACE ON MY
DISK?

TALK TO YOU TOMORROW. I MISSED YOU. PERHAPS IT IS
THE SAME SYNDROME THAT OCCURS IN BATTERED CHIL-
DREN.

ACC41 of 83 Nov 9

Here's something very interesting
and potentially important. The
influential newsletter Satellite
Week (Oct 31) reports on the recent
Geneva TELECOM83:

*Most remarkable satellite exhibit
was 1:100 scale model of concept for
Intelsat I-1A-1, based on space
platform described by Arthur C.
Clarke in his novel "2010," sequel
to "2001." Described as weighing
50,000 kg, measuring 236 x 245m and
assembled in low-earth orbit for
transfer to GEO, modular platform*

---

* Very Large Array. The enormous Y-shaped pattern of radio dishes
in New Mexico—largest in the world, used in the opening of the
movie.

could handle 5 million voice circuits, including one million inter-satellite links and earth-to-moon links. Intelsat said 3 staffers worked for 3 months to define space platform concept. Model, built at cost of $10,000, will be used in forthcoming movie of "2010."

Since I typed that, your PH37 has arrived. Sorry they can't afford a cleaning woman at Arecibo; of course by 2010 it may not be in use anyway. Ditto the VLA--which is certainly an acceptable alternative.

So is the Apollo 11 launch pad--as a museum piece at the 2009 Fortieth Anniversary celebrations. Hey, what about that? Using that (or the VAB*?) would be a nice historic tie-in, and visually just as spectacular.

Does MGM/UA know what our phone bill will be like? When it comes in, will you be washing dishes in the Executive Dining Room? (Where Steve & I lunched last year with Freddie Fields,† Louis Blau,‡ Doug Trumbull§. . . . little did we know. . . .)

---

* Vehicle Assembly Building. The gigantic cube, familiar to all who have watched television from Cape Kennedy, inside which the Apollo spacecraft were assembled.
† President of MGM.
‡ Partner and attorney of Stanley Kubrick.
§ Pioneer of movie special effects who developed many of the techniques used in *2001* and later went on to make his own movies, e.g., *Silent Running* and *Brainstorm*.

PH38. NOVEMBER 9, 1983

WHEN I WALKED INTO THE OFFICE THIS MORNING . . . I SAW THE MOST WONDERFUL PATTERNS ON THE SCREEN HERE. IT LOOKED A LOT LIKE BOWMAN'S FINAL TRIP. I DON'T KNOW WHAT OCCURRED BETWEEN YOU AND THE ATMOSPHERE . . . HOWEVER, IT DIDN'T TAKE A GENIUS TO FIGURE OUT THAT THERE WAS A FILE SOMEWHERE IN THE OZONE LAYER THAT NEVER GOT HERE. I RETRIEVED IT IN SRI LANKA.

I AM GLAD YOU ARE NOT DISAPPOINTED ABOUT ARECIBO. I FEEL SO PASSIONATELY THAT THE OPENING OF THIS FILM HAS TO BE STRIKING. I SIMPLY DON'T WANT TO COMPRO-MISE IT.

AS FAR AS THE PHONE BILL IS CONCERNED . . . I AM SURE YOU WILL BE ABLE TO HEAR THE RUMBLE WHEN THEY GET IT.

THE CASTING SEEMS TO BE GOING WELL. I WILL TELL YOU WHO IS GOING TO PLAY FLOYD AS SOON AS I KNOW. THERE IS AN ACTOR WHO I WANT. I AM TOO SUPERSTITIOUS TO SAY HIS NAME NOW. FOR SOME REASON OR OTHER . . . EVERY ACTOR WANT TO BE IN THIS FILM. THE MOST LIKELY REASON IS THAT NOBODY HAS READ THE SCRIPT.

I WAS THINKING ABOUT YOUR SCHEDULE. I BELIEVE YOU SAID THAT YOU WERE COMING TO WASHINGTON IN THE SPRING. I PLAN ON SHOOTING A BRIEF SCENE IN WASHING-TON IN MAY. IF THAT IS WHEN YOU ARE THERE, IT WOULD BE WONDERFUL. YOU COULD BE AN EXTRA. I MAY SHOOT IN LAFAYETTE PARK. YOU COULD SIT ON A PARK BENCH WITH A BOTTLE OF CHEAP GIN IN A PAPER BAG.

I MAY BE GETTING A CAR OR TWO FROM FORD FOR THE FILM. THEY HAVE SOME PROTOTYPES OF SOME OF THEIR

CARS OF THE FUTURE. IT MIGHT BE NICE TO HAVE ONE
PUTTER DOWN THE STREET BY MS. FERNANDEZ' HOUSE.

THE FIRST JOVIAN ATMOSPHERE TESTS FROM RICHARD
EDLUND* ARE A BIT MORE THAN PROMISING. WE MAY AC-
TUALLY HAVE SOMETHING HERE.

"2001" WAS ON TELEVISION IN NEW YORK AND LOS AN-
GELES THIS PAST WEEK. THE REACTION WAS PHENOME-
NAL. I . . . OF COURSE . . . AM NOW IN THIS SWOOPING
DECLINE . . . PETRIFIED ABOUT THE IDEA OF BEING COM-
PARED TO KUBRICK . . . WHICH IS A BIT LIKE A DWARF
BEING COMPARED TO A WATUSI. I SPENT A LONG TIME
FEELING THAT I WAS UNWORTHY OF THE TASK OF MAKING
THIS FILM. THEN ABOUT THREE WEEKS AGO I CAME TO A
REALIZATION. I AM THE BEST QUALIFIED DIRECTOR IN
AMERICA TO MAKE "2010" . . . BECAUSE THE PRIME
REQUISITE FOR MAKING THE FILM IS TO BE AN ASSHOLE.

ACC42 of 83 Nov 10

Glad that there's such a rush of
actors to be in the movie. You'll be
able to get them cheap. They may even
pay you for the privilege. Maybe you
should get a new casting couch.

Delighted that "2001" was on TV
again. Would you ask Steve to check
with Scott about my residuals. The
first time this happened I got a big
check. The next time, nothing. I'd
like to know why. . . . Further

---

* Visual effects supervisor on the Star Wars trilogy, "Raiders of the
Lost Ark," and "Ghostbusters."

thoughts on Arecibo. My motto is to
exploit the inevitable. Maybe in
2010 it's been replaced by orbiting
or lunar dishes (N.B. ref. in
movie!), so it could be a nostalgic
bit of history linked to our time.
Scraps of paper blowing round the
dish etc. . . . the general grotti-
ness of a Tardovsky movie, e.g.,
especially "Stalker" (a boring drag
except for the final five minutes of
pure magic—which perhaps appealed
to me because I had something very
similar in Chapter 18 of "Childhood's End").

Alternatively if you're scared they
would lynch you in P.R. for being so
downbeat, as the scene is at sunset
surely you could avoid the general
squalor by dramatic photography.

Before you make any cracks about my
acting, wait until you see me as the
Hanging Judge in "The Village in the
Jungle." (It's on Channel 4 in UK
shortly, and I hope my brother can
grab it. I have a tape from German TV
in which my English is merely subti-
tled but my Sinhalese is dubbed into
German, which is odd but makes
sense.)

PH39. NOVEMBER 10, 1983

THE CASTING NEWS THAT I DIDN'T WANT TO TALK ABOUT IS
GETTING CLOSER TO HAPPENING. I WILL LET YOU KNOW
PROBABLY BY MONDAY.

RICHARD TERRILE AND I HAVE BEEN GOING OVER THE DIS-
COVERY BOARDING SEQUENCE. IT IS TRULY DIFFICULT. IT
TURNS OUT THAT THERE IS ALMOST ONE FULL G AT THE
BALL . . . DUE TO THE SPIN. BRAILOVSKY AND CURNOW
WILL HAVE TO ACTUALLY RAPPEL DOWN FROM THE TOP OF
THE BALL. THEY COULD ACTUALLY BE THROWN AWAY
FROM THE BALL IF THEY ARE NOT TETHERED. THE WHOLE
IDEA COULD BE FRIGHTENING . . . AND AGAIN . . . IT WILL
BE SOMETHING NO ONE HAS EVER SEEN BEFORE. IT IS
GOING TO NEED VERY PRECISE EXPLANATION.

ALSO THE POD BAY ENTRANCE IS GOING TO HAVE TO BE A
LITTLE WEIRD. THE TWO MEN ARE NOT WEIGHTLESS WHEN
THEY ENTER. THERE IS GRAVITY DUE TO THE SPIN. THE
FLOOR IS THE POD BAY DOORS. I WILL HANG THE SPACE
SUIT AT THE WRONG ANGLE . . . FEET TOWARDS THE POD
BAY DOORS. THE BRIDGE WOULD HAVE THE SAME GRAVITY
PROBLEM. UNTIL CURNOW CAN STOP THE SPIN . . . DIS-
COVERY WILL BE A ROTTEN PLACE TO SPEND ANY TIME.

THIS, OF COURSE, MEANS THAT I HAVE TO STAND THE
WHOLE POD BAY ON ITS SIDE . . . WHICH IS NOT SOME-
THING YOU HAVE TO WORRY ABOUT . . . JUST KEEP WRIT-
ING ABOUT LARGE SETS ON THEIR SIDE . . . PEOPLE
WALKING ON THE WALLS . . . AND FISH IN THE LIVING
ROOM. NO PROBLEM. ENJOY YOUR GRAPE-NUTS, AND
HAVE LUNCH WITH PRESIDENTS . . . WHILE I AND SEVEN
HUNDRED STAGEHANDS LIFT THE GODDAMNED POD BAY AT
THE COUNT OF THREE. NO PROBLEM.

ACC43 of 83 Nov 11

Slightly disconcerted to see that "2010" has been knocked back to No 2 on the London Sunday Times best-seller list for 6 November by, believe it or not, something called "The Secret Diary of Adrian Mole Aged 13 3/4" by Sue Townsend (Methuen). I suggest you rush out and buy the movie rights.

Re your problems in shooting sideways and upside down in variable gravitational fields: you needn't stick slavishly to the novel as long as the situation is technically correct and valid.

PH40. NOVEMBER 11, 1983

IF YOU TRIED TO REACH ME . . . I AM SORRY. I WAS ON THE MODEL STAGE ALL AFTERNOON. I JUST GOT BACK. IT IS 7:30 HERE NOW.

THE MODELS ARE TURNING INTO SOMETHING SPECIAL. I THINK THEY FINALLY UNDERSTAND THE DESIGNS . . . WHICH ARE UNLIKE ANYTHING THEY HAVE EVER DEALT WITH BEFORE.

I HAVE A QUESTION ABOUT GEOGRAPHY. IN THE DISCOVERY FLIGHT DECK . . . THERE IS A SMALL WHITE PADDED CORRIDOR BEHIND THE PILOT AND CO-PILOT SEATS. THERE IS A LADDER GOING UP ON THE SIDE OF THE CORRIDOR. I WANT TO KNOW HOW BOWMAN AND POOL GET TO THE POD BAY . . . WHICH IS UNDERNEATH THE FLIGHT

DECK. THERE SEEMS TO BE NO ACCESSWAY GOING DOWN.
DO YOU KNOW . . . OR IS THIS SOMETHING THAT ONLY
STANLEY KNOWS.

I WILL BE IN THE STUDIO ALL SATURDAY AND SUNDAY . . .
SO I WILL LEAVE MY MACHINE ON. I WON'T BOTHER YOU
OVER THE WEEKEND . . . UNLESS YOU WANT ME TO.

PH41. NOVEMBER 14, 1983

I HAVE SIGNED ROY SCHEIDER TO PLAY FLOYD. THIS IS NOT
FOR PUBLICATION . . . HOWEVER, IT IS OFFICIAL. I AM
THRILLED. ROY IS EXACTLY THE ACTOR I HAD IN MIND. OUR
FILM HAS JUST TAKEN A SIGNIFICANT STEP FORWARD.

I WAS HERE ALL WEEKEND. I NEVER TRIED CONTACTING
YOU OUT OF FEAR THAT YOU DID NOT HAVE YOUR MACHINE
ON . . . AND THE TELEPHONE RINGING WOULD WAKE YOU
UP. I FIND THAT THE WEEKENDS HERE ARE THE BEST TIMES
TO WRITE AND STUDY.

I HAVE BEEN DEALING WITH YOUR FRIEND RICHARD HOAG-
LAND'S* INFOWHATEVERITIS. IF THERE IS A LOCAL NUM-
BER IN SRI LANKA FOR YOU TO DEAL WITH . . . WHICH IS
SOMETHING THEY ARE GETTING THE ANSWER ON . . . THIS
SYSTEM MAY BE PERFECT FOR US.† IT MIGHT BE MUCH
LESS EXPENSIVE . . . YOU WON'T HAVE TO LEAVE YOUR
MACHINE TURNED ON ALL NIGHT LONG, THEREBY CAUSING
POWER FAILURES ALL OVER ASIA . . . AND I WON'T SPEND
AN ENTIRE NIGHT, AS I DID LAST FRIDAY, BEING UNABLE TO

---

* Science advisor and author of many articles on space and astronomical subjects. As I acknowledge in *2010,* he was the first to suggest that there might be life on Europa.
† This refers to the special low-rate circuits available in most parts of
the world, through which computers can talk to each other cheaply.
We are still looking for one in Sri Lanka.

MAKE A TELEPHONE CONNECTION TO YOU. I WILL FIND OUT
MORE ABOUT IT.

I TOO GO INTO WITHDRAWAL PANGS WHEN WE ARE OUT OF
CONTACT.

ACC45 of 83 Nov 15

Delighted to hear about RS. He's a
magnificent and memorable actor--I
was enormously impressed by "All
That Jazz."

Sorry I can't answer your question
about Discovery's geography. The
man who would know is Frederick I
Ordway III.* He has all the drawings, designs, etc. that he and
Harry Lange† made. (Harry's last
project was "Dark Crystal"--I don't
know where he is now.) Sorry I don't
have his phone number--Fred Durant
will know. (Fred and Pip D. are my
oldest and dearest friends in the
US; he was Assistant Director of the
National Air and Space Museum and
can tell you *anything* about astro-
nautics.)

Just off to have dinner with half the
Cabinet and the Secretary General of

---

* Authority on the history of space travel and author of many books
on the subject. He was technical advisor on *2001*.
† German-born artist who worked with Dr. von Braun's Huntsville
team and later joined the *2001* team in England during the production of the movie..

the Commonwealth. Should be interesting.

PH42. NOVEMBER 15, 1983

I TOLD ROY SCHEIDER OF YOUR HAPPINESS. HE WAS
THRILLED. (HE HASN'T BEEN YELLED AT BY YOU YET.)

THE LEONOV IS GROWING IN SIZE AND DETAIL ON THE
STAGE. THIS IS ALWAYS ONE OF THE MOST THRILLING
PARTS OF FILM. RIGHT NOW . . . EVERYTHING IS POTEN-
TIAL. YOUR MIND CAN FILL IN THE BLANKS. SOMETIMES I
THINK IT IS DOWNHILL FROM HERE.

WHAT DID YOU AND THE SECRETARY GENERAL HAVE FOR
DINNER?

ACC46 of 83 Nov 16

Secretary-General Ramphal (now on
his way to the Commonwealth Conference which the Queen is opening in
Delhi next week) promptly endeared
himself to me by saying he'd just
bought "2010" at the airport. But I
doubt if he will have time to read
it, as he's now busy sending rude
notes to the Turks about Cyprus. He
complained that they've upset his
agenda.

ACC46a of 83 Nov 16

Hey--did you know we were *both* on "That's Entertainment" last night (in Florida, at least) talking about the movie??!! I've no idea what footage they could have found of mine . . .

If you can get hold of a VHS tape I'd like to see it. (I can play your miserable US NTSC--"Never the same color twice"--standard on my machine.)

Now a vast packing case has arrived at the University with my 5-metre satellite ground station and I expect a horde of engineers to install it on the roof. You'll be able to shoot the opening sequence here with a snorkel camera and a bit of ingenuity.

Someone from Time called last night but missed me. If they want to know about the movie I'll head them off at the pass.

I'm afraid this is turning into a ''My Day'' column, but here's another item, the point of which will eventually emerge . . . I'm now surrounded by computer engineers putting modems on the Archives, Kaypro and IBM, so I have backups on the backups.

I've just dropped a note to IBM's chief scientist Louis Branscomb

pointing out that the optical link
used on the PCjr is in "Imperial
Earth" (1976).

PH44. NOVEMBER 18, 1983

I DON'T THINK THERE ARE ANY RUSSIANS IN MOSCOW.
THEY HAVE ALL BEEN IN MY OFFICE FOR THE PAST TWO
WEEKS. I'M SURE THE CIA IS TRYING TO FIGURE OUT WHAT
I'M UP TO. IT'S VERY HARD TO FAKE A CONVINCING RUS-
SIAN ACCENT . . . SO I HAVE BEEN SEEING EVERY RUSSIAN
ACTOR IN CALIFORNIA. THERE ARE SOME SUPRISINGLY
GOOD ONES.

THE LEONOV STARTED TO LOOK LIKE THE LEONOV THIS
WEEK. THE WALLS CAME TOGETHER. I HAVE DESIGNED ALL
CEILINGS AT SEVEN FEET. THE CLAUSTROPHOBIA IS AP-
PARENT EVEN IN THE UNFINISHED SETS. THE LAST FACET
OF THESE SETS IS THE FINISH . . . THE PANELS . . . THE
GIZMOS . . . ALL OF THE SYD MEADIAN DETAILING. THAT
WILL TAKE ANOTHER MONTH AT LEAST. HOWEVER, THE
SHAPES ARE THERE NOW . . . AND I THINK THAT I MAY
HAVE MADE A COUPLE OF PROPER CHOICES.

I WILL BE IN ALL WEEKEND AGAIN. I WILL LEAVE MY MA-
CHINE ON . . . IN CASE YOU ARE FOOLISH ENOUGH TO BE
WORKING.

ACC49 of 83 Nov 19

Now to PH44. If the CIA hangs you up
by your thumbs I'll ask Vernon

Walters to intercede. I'm sure he
still has enough influence to get
you lowered to the ground for five
minutes every hour. (Of course you
can say you are too busy and let them
take Steve.)

I'll get this off now and will remain
in ANS most of the w.e. while you're
at the office, in case you are in a
masochistic mood. (So why else would
you be in movies?)

PH46. NOVEMBER 21, 1983

OUR 2010 TRAILER IS PLAYING WITH BARBRA STREI-
SAND'S NEW FILM "YENTL." I TOLD MGM THAT "YENTL"
IS THE TWO-HOUR ACCOMPANIMENT TO OUR TRAILER. AT
ANY RATE . . . "YENTL" IS A FINE FILM . . . AND IS AT-
TRACTING LARGE AUDIENCES . . . WHICH IS GOOD FOR US.
I RECIEVED A NUMBER OF REPORTS OVER THE WEEKEND
THAT THE AUDIENCES WENT CRACKERS OVER THE
TRAILER. THIS IS ALSO GOOD FOR US. IT ONLY MAKES ME
MORE FRIGHTENED . . . HOWEVER, IT DOES MEAN THAT
THERE IS A LARGE AUDIENCE OUT THERE WITH HIGH EX-
PECTATIONS.

THE NEXT BATCH OF JUPITER TESTS LOOKS GOOD. I ALSO
SAW SOME CLOSE ATMOSPHERE TESTS FROM RICHARD
EDLUND. THEY ARE FURTHER ALONG THAN I THOUGHT.

THE BIG BALLUTE IS OFF THE DRAWING BOARD. JPL LOVES
IT . . . BOEING AEROSPACE LOVES IT . . . SYD MEAD

LOVES IT . . . EVERYONE LOVES IT. I THINK IT LOOKS IN-
SANE . . . WHICH IS WHY IT IS PROBABLY PERFECT.

ACC52 of 83 Nov 22

We got cut off as I was receiving a
call from Walter Cronkite's son
Chip, at a local hotel. Funny--I had
the feeling all the time I was talking to Chip that you could hear and
so would understand what was happening, just as when one is on two
phones at once . . . we have a lot to
learn about this new medium.

That's about it, apart from the UFO
that's just landed on the lawn.

Press conference at the ACC tomor-
row--first of the American engineers (a Jesuit priest!).

ACC53 of 83 Nov 23

The press conference went extremely
well--it was the first time I'd seen
the Arthur Clarke Centre virtually
complete and I was stunned; so was
everyone else. All the locals turned
up--plus TASS representative Valeriy Vasilov! This was a bit of ser-
endipity as satellite engineer and

modern art expert Fr. Lee Lubbers, S.J., had just arrived ahead of the main US team and he specialises in using an Apple to track the (non-stationary) USSR Molniya satellites, used extensively for Russian lessons on his campus, Creighton University, Omaha, Nebraska. So he and Valeriy really hit it off. Instant friendship between Society of Jesus and TASS! (Echoes of 2010, for that matter. . . .)

The 25-foot dish for the Centre has arrived and we hope to erect it in the next few days. Even the bits look impressive—like a dinosaur skeleton. Now I greedily await the 16-footer for my house.

ACC54 of 83 Nov 24

Believe it or not, I've just had a good cry over "Raise the Titanic." I've always been fascinated by her; my very first story (luckily destroyed) was about a spaceship of the same name, and I raised her myself in "Imperial Earth." And the best film on the subject, "A Night to Remember," was made by an old and dear friend, Bill Macquitty. So I was very moved by the scenes when the wreck comes to the surface, and sails into New York. They were ex-

traordinarily well done, and I'm
sorry the film was such a flop. (I
suppose you've heard the joke that
it would have been cheaper to lower
the Atlantic.)

It's always interesting to analyse a
movie's failure (or success). My
quick diagnosis: lack of big stars;
plot so stupid and scientifically
absurd that even laymen could sense
there was something wrong with it;
little interaction on the human
level; anticlimactic ending. That
for starters. . . .

PH47. NOVEMBER 25, 1983

THANKSGIVING IS ALWAYS A TERRIBLY EMOTIONAL TIME
FOR ME. I HAVE SO MUCH TO BE GRATEFUL FOR . . . YET IT
FALLS ON THE ANNIVERSARY OF PRESIDENT KENNEDY'S
DEATH AND FUNERAL. I WAS IN COLLEGE AT THE TIME. I
WAS SO DEEPLY PROUD OF BEING AN AMERICAN. I WANTED
TO MAKE THE GREAT DOCUMENTARY. I WAS SO FULL OF
POLITICAL HOPE. THREE YEARS LATER . . . I WOUND UP
WITH A CAMERA OVER MY SHOULDER IN VIETNAM . . .
WONDERING WHAT MY COUNTRY WAS SMOKING.

ON MONDAY . . . THE LEONOV WILL BE TOGETHER ON THE
MODEL STAGE.

ON TUESDAY . . . THE DISCOVERY WILL BE TOGETHER ON
THE MODEL STAGE.

ON WEDNESDAY . . . I MIGHT BE IN GUATEMALA.

ACC55 of 83 Nov 25

US engineers, huge packing cases and massive hardware descending on me. Main party arrives 6 a.m. tomorrow, so I won't be at the airport. I already have what looks like a Martian fighting machine on my roof, and the Iraqui Embassy next door is getting suspicious.

The plan is to erect and get operational two earth stations over the weekend in time for the official opening of the Arthur Clarke Centre on the 30th, when the Director General of UNESCO will be sending greetings live by the Indian Ocean satellite.

The new baby* in the house is due at the same time . . .

Glad that Time liked "Yentl"--but no mention of the trailer . . .

ACC57 of 83 Nov 28

It's been an incredible day. We'd just discovered that the third antenna has been here two weeks--and no one told us. Unfortunately it's in a barge loaded with ammo for the

---

* Tamara Ekanayake, second daughter of Valerie, Australian-born wife of my long-time partner Hector Ekanayake.

police, so we can't get near it. I've
just phoned the Inspector General of
Police and the General of the Army
. . . hostilities expected any minute.

PH48. NOVEMBER 28, 1983

I AM GOING TO THE VLA IN NEW MEXICO TOMORROW . . .
TO SEE IF THAT WILL WORK FOR THE OPENING SEQUENCE.
AS A RESULT . . . I WILL NOT BE IN THE OFFICE UNTIL
WEDNESDAY MORNING. I WILL LEAVE THE MACHINE ON
WHILE I AM GONE. I WILL LET YOU KNOW HOW THE PLACE
LOOKS.

YOU MENTIONED "BLADE RUNNER" AS ONE OF THE TEN
BEST SCIENCE FICTION FILMS OF ALL TIME. ASSUMING
THAT "2001" IS THE BEST . . . WHAT ARE THE OTHER
EIGHT? ONCE I GET PAST "ALIEN" AND "STAR
WARS". . . I AM HARD PRESSED TO COME UP WITH THE
OTHERS. I WOULD LOVE TO KNOW YOUR LIST.

PH49. NOVEMBER 30, 1983

THE VLA IS EXTRAORDINARY. IF I CAN GET THE COOPERA-
TION THAT I NEED . . . IT WILL BE A WONDERFUL LOCATION
FOR THE FILM. I HAVE TO SEND A WRITTEN REQUEST TO
THE DIRECTOR OF THE WHOLE OPERATION. I WILL HAVE
HIS NAME TOMORROW. YOU WILL KNOW WHO HE IS
(Oh. . . Bob. He's a very nice fellow. Both he and
Margaret were here scuba diving in '80. Ask him

if he still has my sweater.) . . . OR SOMETHING LIKE
THAT. IF IN FACT YOU DO KNOW HIM . . . PERHAPS A LIT-
TLE HELP FROM YOU COULD HELP.

THE DEPUTY DIRECTOR OF THE VLA CAME TO MEET ME
WHEN I WAS THERE. HE PRACTICALLY GENUFLECTED. ALL
OF THEM HAVE COPIES OF "2010" BOUND IN LEATHER
WITH "HOLY BIBLE" WRITTEN ON THE FRONT AND
TASSLES COMING OUT THE BOTTOM. HIS NAME IS PETER
SOMETHING . . . HE'S FROM NEW ZEALAND. (Oh . . .
Peter. He's such a nice fellow. He and Sally were
here in '79 scuba diving. Ask him if he still has
my shirt.)

I HOPE EVERYBODY SCRAMBLES OFF YOUR ROOF SOON
. . . AND YOUR LIFE BECOMES MORE TRANQUIL. THIS IS SO
I CAN START DRIVING YOU CRAZY ONCE AGAIN.

PH50. DECEMBER 1, 1983

YOU HAVE BEEN CAUSING A BIT OF A DRAMA. I TRIED TO
TELL YOU YESTERDAY THAT YOU WERE SENDING THE
WRONG FILE TO YOURSELF. STEVE'S FILE IS COOP1 . . .
NOT COOP 1. THERE IS NO SPACE BETWEEN COOP AND 1,
AND THESE STUPID MACHINES ARE VERY STRICT. IN THE
MIDDLE OF YOUR ATTEMPT . . . YOUR MACHINE WENT OFF
THE LINE. I TRIED CALLING YOU BACK . . . EXCEPT YOU
HAD TAKEN YOUR MODEM OFF . . . SO THE TELEPHONE
KEPT ON RINGING . . . AND THERE WAS NO ANSWER.

THIS MORNING . . . I FOUND SOME WRITING ON MY
SCREEN. WHATEVER YOU HAD SENT . . . WAS NOT ON MY
DISK. THE LAST TRANSMISSION THAT I HAVE IS ACC57. I
AM STILL WAITING FOR YOUR TEN BEST LIST. I DON'T KNOW
WHY THERE WAS NOTHING ON THE DISK. I ALSO DON'T
KNOW WHY YOU TOOK YOUR MODEM OFF THE HOOK RIGHT

AFTER YOU TRIED TO SEND YOURSELF THE FILE. SO THIS
MORNING . . . WHEN I FOUND INDICATIONS OF A PHANTOM
FILE . . . I WAS SCARED STIFF TO CONNECT WITH YOUR
MACHINE, BECAUSE I DIDN'T KNOW IF YOUR MODEM WAS
TURNED ON OR OFF . . . AND I DIDN'T WANT TO WAKE YOU
WITH SOME HORRIBLE RINGING . . . AND CAUSE ALL OF
YOUR WIVES TO FALL OFF THE ROOF.

YOU MAY HAVE BEEN TO THE STARS AND BACK . . . YOU
MAY HAVE UNLOCKED THE SECRETS OF LIFE . . . HOW-
EVER, YOU DON'T WORK THIS STUFF TOO GOOD.

YOUR HUMBLE AND TOTALLY CONFUSED SERVANT.

ACC58 of 83 Nov 29-Dec 1

Here's the rough-cut of my best: I
may change my mind on some, but not
many . . .

"Metropolis"; "Things to Come";
"Frankenstein"; "King Kong" (original); "Forbidden Planet"; "The
Thing" (original); "The Day the
Earth Stood Still"; "2001"; "Star
Wars"; "CE3K" (revised); "Alien";
"Blade Runner." (No way I can make it
ten . . . and I'm still brooding
over Jedi, Kahn, E.T.) Actually it
would make more sense to have two
lists: Most important, and Best.

The London Times says that "The
Right Stuff" is a flop. True? Delighted to see that "2010," after

exactly one year, has jumped back to
No 3 on the Locus* best-seller list--
from No 9 the month before. Wonder
why. "Foundation's Edge"† has
dropped off completely! Have you
seen the new Starlog? Quite pleased
with the interview. I also have a
piece in Analog this month, not yet
received.

Now recovering from an exhausting
week. The Earth Station on my roof is
functioning well, but it will be
some time before the mess of wiring
is sorted out and I learn how to find
all the satellites I can now pick up.
Would you believe that the very
first program we received was a
cricket match in India--broadcast
from a Russian satellite!

The opening of the Arthur Clarke
Centre went very well, and I'm mail-
ing you the special supplement the
local paper put out. The most splendid of the dishes (25 feet!) is in
front of the Centre; a similar one is
being erected on the roof of the University. The local engineers are
learning how to operate them. Last
night we had a dinner and cultural
show for the whole group, which gave
them a very nice send-off.

---

* *The* monthly magazine of the science fiction world, read from cover
to cover by everyone seriously interested in the subject.
† One of the 300-odd books by Isaac What's-His-Name. Between
you and me, some are quite good.

ACC60 of 83 Dec 2

I'm glad the VLA fills the bill, and
am sure the owners will be happy to
co-operate. Tell them I'll auto-
graph their copies of "2010." (Sometimes I have a fantasy of Sothebys'
auctioneer running up the bidding
for a rare unautographed copy.)

Just seen myself on the TV news re-
splendent in purple robes at the
opening of the ACC, with the 25-foot
HERO* dish in the background. It
looks most impressive: if you can't
get the VLA you can hire it on very
reasonable terms.

ACC63 of 83 Dec 5

I certainly did not expect to find
you in the store 6 p.m. Sunday night
and was quite surprised when your
disembodied voice emerged from the
modem. You reacted fine: I calcu-
lated that it would take you just 60
seconds to switch on your system before I called you again . . . we seem
to be getting our machines under

---

* Builders of satellite receiving dishes in Hialeah, Florida, who gen-
erously presented the 25-foot dish to the Arthur C. Clarke Center.

control, touch wood, instead of the
other way round.

Here's my normal schedule, which I
hope to resume now that the invasion
is over:

	S.L. Time	L.A. Time
"bed tea":	06.30*	17.00
open office:	07.00	17.30
close office:	21.30	08.00
go to sleep:	21.31	

*old Sri Lankan custom: ask Steve

As you will see, I have an active social life: however, I do get in an
hour of vicious table tennis at the
local swimming club between 16.00
and 18.00.

My modem *sometimes* (but not always)
prevents other callers getting
through, so I don't want it on during
my office hours. But as you will see
that fits our schedules fine; you
have all day to think of something
rude to spoil my breakfast. And vice
versa.

Roy S: welcome aboard! You've already had two of the great lines in
modern movies: (1) ''You're gonna
need a bigger boat.'' (2) ''I wonder
if Kubrick ever gets depressed.''
Hope we'll give you some more.

PH51. DECEMBER 5, 1983

ROY WAS THRILLED BY YOUR NOTE. I SHOWED HIM THE
SETS AND THE MODELS TODAY. I THINK HE GOT A SENSE
OF HOW MUCH EFFORT IS GOING INTO THIS SILLY ENTER-
PRISE.

I WANT YOUR OPINION ABOUT SOMETHING IMPORTANT. IN
THE FINAL ESCAPE SEQUENCE . . . WHEN HAL IS ASKING A
SERIES OF GOOD QUESTIONS AND CHANDRA* HAS TO LIE
TO HIM . . . WOULDN'T IT BE INTERESTING IF CHANDRA
COULD NOT LIE. SUPPOSE CHANDRA TELLS HAL THE TRUTH
. . . THAT THERE IS A DANGER DISCOVERY COULD BE DE-
STROYED . . . HOWEVER, IF HE DOESN'T HELP . . . AND
THERE WAS DANGER . . . THEN NO ONE COULD SURVIVE.
HAL COULD LOGICALLY CHOOSE TO FIRE THE DISCOVERY
ENGINES AND HELP THEM. ONE . . . BECAUSE IT DOES
MAKE MATHEMATICAL SENSE FOR SOME TO SURVIVE
RATHER THAN NONE AT ALL . . . AND TWO . . . IT COULD
BE A VERY POIGNANT MOMENT. I THINK THIS IS WORTH
THINKING ABOUT. IT COULD PROVIDE AN IMPORTANT CLI-
MAX FOR CHANDRA AND HAL. PLEASE TELL ME WHAT YOU
THINK OF THIS.

PH52. DECEMBER 6, 1983

I SPENT MOST OF THE DAY WITH ROY. IT IS WONDERFUL TO
HEAR HIM START TO READ SOME OF THE SCENES OUT
LOUD. HE HAS THAT MIRACULOUS QUALITY OF MAKING DIA-
LOGUE SOUND BELIEVABLE. HE IS A VERY BRIGHT MAN . . .
AND A VERY KIND ONE.

I READ YOUR NOTE TO HIM. HE WAS ASTOUNDED THAT YOU
HAD REMEMBERED THE KUBRICK LINE. HE HAD FORGOT-
TEN IT.

---

* The inventor of HAL.

THE FULL LEONOV STANDS IN THE MODEL SHOP. EVERY DAY WHEN I WALK IN THERE . . . THE MODEL MAKERS STAND IN TERROR . . . WAITING FOR ME TO COMPLAIN ABOUT SOME MICROSCOPIC DETAIL THAT I DON'T LIKE. I FEEL LIKE SOMETHING OUT OF ''BRIDGE ON THE RIVER KWAI.'' THE OTHER DAY I WALKED IN . . . AND THERE IT WAS . . . ALL MULTI-MILLION PARTS OF IT, WITH THE DOCKING RING SWIVELING . . . AND LIVING QUARTERS RO-TATING. ONLY WHEN YOU LOOKED CLOSELY AT IT . . . COULD YOU SEE THE LITTLE MAN ON THE SURF BOARD THAT THEY HAD PUT ON THE ANTENNA.

PH54. DECEMBER 9, 1983

THERE IS AN OUTSIDE CHANCE THAT THIS SILLY FILM MAY ACTUALLY WORK. I JUST SAW THE SECOND JUPITER TEST FROM WHITNEY. IT IS AN ENHANCED IMAGE OF JUPITER . . . WITH ELEVATION ADDED TO THE CLOUD FORMATIONS. IT IS ASTONISHING. I LOOKED AT IT . . . AND TOLD THEM THAT IT NEEDED A GOOD DEAL OF WORK . . . AND THERE WERE PROBLEMS WITH COLOR . . . HOWEVER, I THOUGHT IT HAD POSSIBILITIES. I LIED THROUGH MY POINTY TEETH. IT IS AMAZING. I SIMPLY DON'T WANT THEM TO KNOW HOW EXCITED I AM.

ROY IS GOING HOME TO NEW YORK THIS WEEKEND. I COULD NOT HAVE FOUND A BETTER ACTOR FOR THE ROLE . . . OR A NICER MAN TO WORK WITH.

ACC68 of 83 Dec 10

Delighted to hear about the Jupiter footage.

PH55. DECEMBER 13, 1983

I AM SORRY ABOUT MY ABSENCE. YESTERDAY WAS ONE OF
THE MORE CHAOTIC CHAPTERS IN A SAGA THAT HAS NOT
BEEN KNOWN FOR ITS SERENITY. YESTERDAY WAS MY
FIRST FULL-SCALE PRODUCTION MEETING. IT IS A WEEKLY
RITUAL THAT I INSIST ON. IT BEGINS EIGHT WEEKS BEFORE
SHOOTING . . . AND OCCURS EVERY MONDAY UNTIL IT'S
TOO LATE. ALL OF MY DEPARTMENT HEADS (SPECIAL EF-
FECTS, ART, MAKEUP, PROPS, ETC.) SIT AROUND A CON-
FERENCE TABLE. I GO OVER EACH DAY OF THE SHOOTING
SCHEDULE WITH THEM . . . AND ASK A SERIES OF QUES-
TIONS. THEY ARE SUPPOSED TO HAVE THE ANSWERS BY
THE NEXT MEETING. THE FIRST MEETING IS NORMALLY
DREADFUL . . . AND THIS ONE WAS NO EXCEPTION.
TWENTY BLANK FACES . . . STARING HELPLESSLY BACK
AT ME . . . ALL SAYING THINGS LIKE . . . ''YOU WANT ONE
MAN WALKING ON THE SIDE OF A WALL WHILE THE OTHER
MAN IS ON THE FLOOR AND ALL OF THE MONITORS ARE
GOING TO HAVE GRAPHIC PROGRAMS IN THEM AND A LIVE
TELEVISION IMAGE OF JUPITER IS ON THE MAIN CONSOLE
AND THERE IS GOING TO BE DIALOGUE DURING THE SCENE
AND YOU WANT TO DO THIS WHEN ARE YOU OUT OF YOUR
MIND?''

IT DOESN'T BUILD CONFIDENCE. IT DOES CONVINCE ME
THAT THERE ISN'T A CHANCE TO GET THIS THING DONE IN
TIME. MY ONLY SOLACE IS THAT I GO THROUGH THIS FEEL-
ING EVERY TIME I START A FILM.

I HAVE FOUND FIVE BRILLIANT RUSSIAN ACTORS. NONE OF
THEM HAVE BEEN IN THIS COUNTRY MORE THAN FOUR
YEARS. THEY WERE ALL VERY SUCCESSFUL IN THE SOVIET
UNION. MOST OF THEM JUST COMPLETED A FILM* HERE

---

* Moscow on the Hudson

THAT WAS DIRECTED BY A VERY TALENTED MAN NAMED
PAUL MAZURSKY. OUR LEONOV CREW IS NOT AS FAMOUS
AS OUR AMERICAN CREW.

PH56. DECEMBER 14, 1983

I HEARD FROM MY ASSISTANT . . . WHO EVIDENTLY HEARD
FROM STEVE THAT YOU MAY IN FACT GET OUT TO CALIFOR-
NIA NEXT YEAR. I REMEMBER ONE OF YOUR FILES THAT
SAID YOU COULDN'T COME. IS THERE A CHANCE?

MY WASHINGTON DATES WILL BE IN THE MIDDLE OF MAY.
WHEN ARE YOU SCHEDULED TO GET YOUR AWARD?

ACC69 of 83 Dec 14

I've written to Del Rey about the
lack of reference to the movie on the
paperback. However, the splendid
publicity poster has a big splash
("2010 to be a major motion picture!
Film rights have been sold to
MGM/UA, the company that made
2001!")--so you can't say that they
are trying to keep it a secret.

A couple of coincidences: tuned into
the Raduga satellite* the other
morning and there was a big press

---

* Russian direct broadcast satellite, which gives excellent pictures
with a receiving antenna less than ten feet in diameter.

conference in progress, featuring
cosmonaut Lyakov, just safely back
to earth. A year or so ago he'd been
riding the Hovercraft on my lawn.

ACC70 of 83 Dec 14

Glad you've found your Russians.

Now off to British Council cocktail
party--I have to reassure my compa-
triots from time to time that I have
not gone native. I shall wear my sa-
rong.

PH57. DECEMBER 15, 1983

THE DOLPHIN SITUATION IS HOPELESS. WE CANNOT BUILD
A SUITABLE HOUSE TO ACCOMMODATE A TANK. THE
WHOLE THING WOULD COST ABOUT HALF A MILLION DOL-
LARS. MY NEXT THOUGHT IS TO HAVE CAROLINE BE IN-
VOLVED IN TEACHING A HIGHLAND GORILLA TO SIGN. IN
THE FIRST PLACE . . . I THINK IT IS A WONDERFUL PRO-
FESSION. SECONDLY . . . I LOVE YOUR CONCEPT OF HER
INVOLVED IN TRYING TO MAKE THAT KIND OF CONTACT
WITH ANOTHER SPECIES. THIRDLY . . . A HIGH MOUNTAIN
GORILLA IS AN ANIMAL THAT ONE NEVER SEES IN A FILM.
AS A MATTER OF FACT THERE HAS NEVER BEEN ONE IN A
FILM. EVERY TIME A GORILLA IS CALLED FOR . . . WE AL-
WAYS SEE A MAN IN A GORILLA SUIT. NO MATTER HOW
ELABORATE THE SUIT IS . . . IT IS STILL A MAN IN A GO-

RILLA SUIT. AS A RESULT . . . THE PROPORTIONS ARE WRONG . . . THE MOUTH IS WRONG . . . THE EYES ARE WRONG . . . THE FEET ARE WRONG . . . AND THEY CAN NEVER HAVE THE STRENGTH OR THE AGILITY TO DO CERTAIN THINGS. I AM WORKING ON A SECRET IDEA. I AM WORKING WITH PEOPLE HERE WHO USE APES IN FILMS. ONE OF THEM IS A VERY LARGE ORANGUTAN. WE HAVE DEVELOPED A METHOD TO USE MAKEUP AND PROSTHETICS ON THE ORANG . . . TURNING HIM INTO A SILVERBACK GORILLA. SOME OF THE EARLY RESULTS ARE ASTONISHING. YOU KNOW YOU ARE DEALING WITH A GORILLA . . . NOT A MAN. ASIDE FROM THE OBVIOUS PROPORTIONAL AND ATHLETIC DIFFERENCES . . . HE DOES THINGS WITH HIS FEET . . . AND HIS MOUTH AND TONGUE . . . THAT A HUMAN COULD NEVER DO. I AM GOING TO DO MORE TESTING. I WILL SEND YOU A PHOTOGRAPH WHEN WE FINISH THE MAKEUP. BEFORE I GO ANY FURTHER . . . I WOULD LIKE YOUR OPINION OF THIS. IF YOU HATE IT . . . I WON'T SPEND ALL THE TIME AND EFFORT TO SEE WHAT HAPPENS. IF YOU LIKE IT . . . I WILL PROCEED. LASTLY . . . IF YOU REALLY DO HATE THE IDEA . . . I WILL TELL THE ORANG THAT YOU COST HIM HIS JOB.

ACC71 of 83 Dec 15

My US trip depends entirely on President Reagan. We're waiting for the White House to agree a date for the Marconi Award ceremony. If not at the White House, it may be at the Academy of Science. In any case it will be late Spring. I have to give an address saying what I have done with the loot. I will try to work in a

plug for the movie, if I can think of
any possible way the President might
be interested in such matters.

I had wistfully dreamed of sneaking
quietly in and out of Washington so I
could hurry across and see what you
are doing to my poor little book.
This naive hope has now been dashed
by a cable from the Sri Lanka Embassy: "Arthur Clarke Foundation of
US will meet shortly to plan operational strategy . . . Executive
Director Frederick C Durant III
(Retired Deputy Director of Space
Museum) . . . Senior Special Advisor Hon. Abbott Washburn . . . Ar-
range Symposium Spring 84 to
coincide with Arthur Clarke's visit
with Smithsonian collaboration--
theme satellite communications for
developing world co-sponsors IEEE,
AAS and AIAA . . ." and so on . . .
Well--what arrives at L.A. after
this may look like one of the survi-
vors of the Donner party. And I have
to get back to SL by May 21 to start
shooting the 13 episodes of "Strange
Powers." But I'm sure we'll work out
something, and of course I'm dying
to meet you all and to see what's
happening.

Feeling homesick. Charles Sheffield (Vice President Earth Satellite Corp and excellent s.f. writer)
has just sent me his company's latest computer-processed Landsat

image of SW England. I think I can
see our farm . . .

___

Sorry--the only substitute I'll accept for my dolphins is a pet giant
squid.

Here's an idea. Walk down the corridor and do a deal with Bob Radnitz,
who has been trying to film "Dolphin
Island" for fifteen years and has
done all the homework. He could use
the same set, so MGM/UA would have
two movies for the price of 1¼. Did
you know I was a financial genius as
a result of five years in H.M. Exche-
quer and Audit Dept? Oh well--give
Bob my regards anyway . . .

Seriously:

Next to the elephant, the Bengal
tiger, and possibly some denizens of
Muscle Beach, the silverback is the
most superb of land animals. The
orang, on the other hand, is a sweet
wistful comic, and I find it incredible that even Stuart Freeborn*
could disguise it as a gorilla but
I'll be fascinated to see your
photos. However, my general reac-

___

* The makeup genius responsible for the ape-men in *2001*—and for
aging Bowman in the final sequence.

tion is negative because (a) there will be confusing resonances to the opening of "2001" and you will arouse expectations that will be disappointed; (b) this is only background and plays no part in the story line (unless you make a change--worth thinking about?).

Roger Caras and I visited all the great apes (see "Lost Worlds of 2001"), and I have also met Roger Fouts* and his friends (Washoe etc.) in Oklahoma. So I'm certainly sympathetic in principle and would be happy if it works out.

But make sure your orang has a green card and isn't a wetback.

PH58. DECEMBER 16, 1983

I DON'T WANT TO USE THE ORANG/GORILLA.

I STILL CAN'T DO THE DOLPHIN . . . RADNITZ NOTWITH-STANDING. ROGER SUGGESTED PENGUINS. HE HAS SOME-ONE AT SEA WORLD IN SAN DIEGO THAT I WILL CONTACT. PENGUINS IN THE HOUSE SOUND INTERESTING . . . ESPE-CIALLY IF I CAN GET THE ONES WITH THE LONG YELLOW HEADDRESS . . . THE ONES WHO LOOK LIKE STERLING HOLLOWAY. YOU DON'T LIKE GORILLAS IN THE HOUSE . . . SO IS IT POSSIBLE THAT A PENGUIN STRIKES YOUR FANCY?

---

* Scientist who has made a speciality of ape languages. The chimpanzee Washoe is perhaps his most famous client. He was involved as an advisor on ape behavior in the excellent movie *Greystoke: The Legend of Tarzan.*

STEVE WISHES YOU A HAPPY BIRTHDAY. I DIDN'T KNOW IT WAS YOUR BIRTHDAY. I WOULD HAVE SENT YOU SOMETHING IF I HAD KNOWN, HOWEVER, I DIDN'T KNOW, SO YOU GET NOTHING.

I WILL BE IN THE OFFICE TOMORROW (SATURDAY), SO IF YOU CARE TO GIVE ME YOUR PENGUIN OPINION, I WOULD BE GRATEFUL.

HAPPY BIRTHDAY. YOU BLEW A GREAT PRESENT.

ACC73 of 83 Dec 17

Damn--I had just written you a marvellous outline in which the gorilla is the real cause of the Floyds' estrangement, Heywood's suspicions having been growing steadily ever since Chris was born covered with hair from head to foot.

Frankly I have no feelings about penguins one way or the other, my only acquaintaince with them being limited to a single species. In 1955 I was on a small island a hundred miles south of Sydney; here's the quote from the long o/p "Coast of Coral," Chapter 5. "Bowen Island also supports a colony of minute but

extremely bad-tempered penguins,
standing about nine inches high.
These are so pretty and so easily
caught . . . that it is hard to resist picking them up. They then
belie their attractive appearance
by cursing madly and removing all
accessible pieces of hand with their
needle-sharp beaks."

Penguins may be distractingly comic
(do you remember "The Man Who Came To
Dinner"?)—though the bigger ones
are handsome and dignified, like
old-style British butlers.

Again, I feel you shouldn't waste
time and effort on this unless something really clicks with you. If you
want to stress the communications
aspect, what about bees (cf. von
Frisch*) or termites. (TV infrared
microsopes watching them could be
fascinating and unfamiliar. And a
lot cheaper than dolphins.) Did you
ever see Wolper's "Helstrom Chroni-
cle"? or Saul Bass' "Phase Four"?
  The "Encyclopaedia of SF" says that
the latter was too consciously mod-
elled on "2001"—I'd never thought
of that.

If you merely want a spectacular animal there are the big cats and
snakes; doubtless Roger has many
other suggestions.

---

* Scientist who first discovered the "dance" language of bees.

By 2010 there will be a lot of electronic animal-tutors-companions around as child's playmates (cf. "Blade Runner"). What about disguising a real animal as a mechanical one?

Someone breeds horses about 2 feet high. This I'd like to see. What about a small dinosaur? The geneticists may have engineered some by 2010.

Just trying to be helpful. Isn't it lucky I'm on the other side of the world. You'd be even better off if the speed of light was only five miles an hour.

The country is just closing down for three days. Holy Prophet's Birthday today, Sunday tomorrow, Poya Monday . . . All we need is Yom Kippur on Tuesday. I'll be here and will peek at your directory from time to time between screening the Kennedy TV series, which looks stunning.

PH60. DECEMBER 19, 1983

I AM GOING NUTS TRYING TO SOLVE THIS FLOYD HOUSE-HOLD PROBLEM. I GATHER FROM YOUR LETTER THAT PENGUINS DON'T THRILL YOU. I DID SOME MORE CHECKING ABOUT DOLPHINS . . . AND FOUND THAT EVEN IF WE FOUND A PERFECT HOUSE . . . THERE IS ALMOST NO CHANCE OF EVER GETTING CLEARANCE TO SHIP A DOL-

PHIN. MY NEXT THOUGHT IS TO BREAK THE SEQUENCE UP
INTO TWO PARTS, THAT IS . . . START OUT WITH CAROLINE
AT WORK . . . IN A TANK WITH A DOLPHIN. PERHAPS
CHRISTOPHER COULD BE WITH HER. INSTEAD OF FLOYD
WITH THEM AT DINNER . . . HE COULD SHOW UP AT HER
PLACE OF WORK TO TELL HER. IF WE ARE GOING TO EVEN
HAVE THE SLIGHTEST CHANCE OF A DOLPHIN . . . I THINK
THAT IS THE ONLY WAY. PLEASE TELL ME YOUR REACTION.

I HAD MY SECOND PRODUCTION MEETING TODAY. THE RE-
SULTS WERE ABOUT AS CHAOTIC AS THE FIRST ONE.

ACC75 of 83 Dec 20

Here's a quote I've just found: "I
enjoy working with someone I find
stimulating. One of the most fruit-
ful and enjoyable collaborations I
have had was with Arthur C Clarke in
writing "2001." . . . One of the
paradoxes of movie writing is that,
with a few notable exceptions, writers who can really write are not interested in working on film scripts.
They quite correctly regard their
important work as being done for
publication." Hear, hear . . .

Really, I've no feelings one way or
the other: the dolphins, much as I
love them, were merely local color
and didn't contribute to the story.
I still find it amazing that you
can't work out something with Sea
World. At least you could shoot a se-

quence there with Mrs F and Chris interacting with dolphins, if you feel this makes sense.

PH61. DECEMBER 20, 1983

WE MAY BE GETTING SOME COOPERATION FROM MARINE-LAND . . . WHICH IS IN THE LOS ANGELES AREA. I WILL PROBABLY BE ABLE TO SHOOT IN ONE OF THEIR TRAINING TANKS. THE CHANCE OF GETTING A DOLPHIN TRANS-PORTED OUT OF THE FACILITY ARE VERY SLIM.

I TURNED THE LIGHTS ON IN THE LEONOV SET TODAY FOR THE FIRST TIME. IT WAS NICE TO SEE EVERYONE'S REAC-TION . . . WHICH WAS ONE OF AWE. THERE IS A SPIRIT HERE AMONG THE CONSTRUCTION AND SPECIAL EFFECTS CREWS THAT I HAVE NEVER ENCOUNTERED BEFORE. THEY ARE ALL CRAZED OVER THE CHALLENGE OF BUILDING SETS THAT BREAK THE MOLD, AND ARE SO AMBITIOUS. THEY ARE ALL POSSESSIVE ABOUT THEM. WHEN I TURNED THE LIGHTS ON TODAY . . . YOU COULD SEE THEIR EXCITE-MENT. I FEEL THAT THERE IS AN ENORMOUS AMOUNT OF WORK NEEDED TO GET THESE SETS TO WHERE I WANT THEM. HOWEVER, I WOULD BE LYING IF I DID NOT TELL YOU THAT IT LOOKS ENCOURAGING.

I AM ALMOST FULLY CAST NOW. I HAVE NOTHING TO COM-PLAIN ABOUT IN THAT AREA.

AS FAR AS YOUR QUOTE FROM KUBRICK GOES . . . I THINK THAT BOTH OF YOU WERE FORTUNATE TO WORK WITH EACH OTHER . . . AND THE RESULTS ARE PROOF OF THAT UNION. OUR COLLABORATION IS OBVIOUSLY LESS STIMU-LATING FOR YOU. I AM LESS TALENTED THAN STANLEY . . . HOWEVER, I AM A BIGGER PAIN IN THE ASS.

ACC76 of 83 Dec 21

TASS was here this morning and I told
them that you have some of the best
Russian actors outside the SU. "Why
not inside?" "Really," I answered,
"Can you imagine a US–USSR movie
collaboration at the present moment? Look at the problems on "Gorky
Park." We may already be in trouble
in the US as it is for being pro-Rus-
sian . . ."

Glad that Marineland looks promising. And Leonov.

I haven't touched "Songs" since August, even though it's completely
worked out and there are at least
20,000 words in Archie. I've no idea
when I'll have time even to think
about it again—perhaps when I get
back from the US. Rather frustrating, as I'm sure it will be my best
book.

PH62. DECEMBER 21, 1983

NO NEWS FROM THE DOLPHIN FRONT.

MUCH OF THIS DAY WAS SPENT DESIGNING EVA HELMETS.
SPACE SUITS ARE HORRIBLE THINGS TO DESIGN FOR FILM
WORK. IN THE FIRST PLACE, A LOT OF WORK IS DONE BY
ACTORS HANGING FROM WIRES FOR EVA SEQUENCES.

WIRE WORK IS DIFFICULT ENOUGH WITHOUT ADDING THE
WEIGHT AND BULK OF A SUIT. SECONDLY, AFTER "CAPRI-
CORN ONE" AND "OUTLAND," I AM GETTING TIRED OF
WATCHING MY CAST TURN BLUE AND KEELING OVER FROM
A LACK OF AIR. VENTILATION AND COOLING SYSTEMS
MUST BE MINIATURIZED TO FIT IN THE BACKPACKS. THEN
WE HAVE THE HELMETS. THEY HAVE TO FUNCTION. THEY
CANNOT LOOK LIKE HELMETS THAT WE HAVE SEEN BE-
FORE. I WANT THEM TO HAVE EXTERIOR LIGHTS. THE
FACEPLATES WILL REFLECT EVERY DAMN LIGHT ON THE
SOUND STAGE. THOSE ARE JUST SOME OF THE PROB-
LEMS. I WANT YOU TO FEEL SORRY FOR ME. THAT IS THE
ONLY REASON FOR MY COMPLAINTS.

THE DISCOVERY IS STARTING TO LOOK LIKE THE DISCOV-
ERY. IT IS EERIE TO SEE IT. I ALSO GO INTO GREAT SWOOP-
ING DECLINES EVERY TIME I LOOK AT THAT BALL . . . AND
REALIZE WHAT I AM FOLLOWING. AS I SAID BEFORE . . .
THE ONLY THING THAT KEEPS ME GOING . . . IS THE REALI-
ZATION THAT THE PRIME QUALITY NEEDED TO DIRECT THIS
FILM, AFTER STANLEY'S WAS SO BRILLIANT, IS TO BE AN
ASSHOLE. AS A RESULT . . . I AM EMINENTLY QUALIFIED.

ACC77 of 83 Dec 22

Not a thing to report . . . except
that "Capricorn One" is on British
TV tonight and I hope you get a piece
of the action.

ACC78 of 83 Dec 23

There's a news item in today's paper
which has given me a very strange
feeling.

In February 1962 I became completely
paralysed (total basket case).
There was a polio epidemic on in the
country at the time and Dr Sabin* was
here to advise. A London specialist
said I had polio, but the local man
insisted that I was suffering from a
lesion of the spinal cord in the neck
area. They would never agree but I
feel that the latter was right. (See
"The Treasure of the Great Reef" for
boring details.)

Well--this morning I read that poor
Dr Sabin is himself paralysed--
owing to a lesion of the spinal cord
in the neck! Millions of people will
feel sad about this. I hope he makes
as good a recovery as I did.

PH63. DECEMBER 27, 1983

STEVE JUST BROUGHT ME SOME PHOTOGRAPHS OF YOU IN
A TEE-SHIRT . . . STANDING UNDERNEATH A GIANT UM-
BRELLA. IT IS ALL VERY IMPRESSIVE. DOES THAT DISH EN-
ABLE YOU TO GET THE F.A. CUP? IF NOT . . . THEN IT
STRIKES ME AS A WASTE OF MONEY. MORE IMPRESSIVE

---

* Dr. Albert Bruce Sabin, developer of the oral polio vaccine named
after him.

THAN THE DISH . . . IS THE PHOTOGRAPH OF YOU IN YOUR CHANCELLOR ROBES. YOU LOOK POSITIVELY PAPAL.

THERE IS NOT A LOT TO REPORT. TOMORROW IS THE NEXT PRODUCTION MEETING. I LOOK FORWARD TO IT. I LOVE TO HEAR GROWN MEN LIE.

ACC81 of 83 Dec 28

Japanese Playboy here all day, doing a story on my "electronic cottage." Well, at last count there were eight computers littering up the place. I'll pretend that I'm talking to you through my 5-metre dish. (We've now located 7 USSR satellites.) Talking of Playboy, Hef's Xmas card has just arrived and I find it rather sad. Foreground dominated by his pipe, the only girls a couple of small angels in the background—fully dressed, yet. Maybe advancing years have brought him round to Kipling's viewpoint: "A woman is only a woman, but a good cigar is a smoke." His rival Bob Guccione's (and Kathy Keeton's)* card also arrived today. It features a fine Renoir. Not any old Renoir—theirs. Beat that . . .

---

* Publishers of *Penthouse* and *Omni* magazines.

ACC82 of 83 Dec 29

All my 5-metre Paraclipse dish
brings me at the moment is boring
cricket from India, courtesy of
Russian satellites. But the match is
now over, thank heavens, and there
may be something more interesting.
We're still exploring the orbit and
logging in new comsats.

ACC83 of 83 Dec 30

Don't even mention SDE--I've not
been able to give it a thought since
July, and only the curfew and absence of mail during the riots allowed to me to do anything this year.
I am completely exhausted mentally
just coping with mail and visitors
--over twenty friends or friends of
friends circulating in the island at
the moment.

PH64. JANUARY 2, 1984

HAPPY NEW YEAR. I PASSIONATELY HOPE THAT MR. OR-
WELL TURNS OUT TO BE WRONG. PERHAPS OUR FILM WILL
MAKE EVERYONE THINK . . . AND GIVE THEM SOME HOPE.

PH65. JANUARY 3, 1984

THIS IS THE DAY AFTER THE ROSE BOWL . . . WHICH HAS NOTHING TO DO WITH ROSES OR FINE CHINA. IT IS A FOOTBALL GAME AND A PARADE . . . ATTENDED BY MORE THAN ONE MILLION PEOPLE. THE WEATHER WAS GLORIOUS . . . WHICH IS A CALAMITY. EVERY WINTER . . . WHEN THE REST OF THE NATION IS IN SUB-ZERO WEATHER . . . GOD PLAYS ONE OF HIS LITTLE PRACTICAL JOKES ON CALIFORNIA. THE DAY THE ROSE BOWL IS TELEVISED . . . THE SKY IS CLEAR BLUE . . . AND THE TEMPERATURE IS IN THE SEVENTIES. (YESTERDAY IT WAS IN THE EIGHTIES.) NATURALLY THE REST OF AMERICA TAKES ONE LOOK AT THIS, AND DECIDES TO MOVE OUT HERE. MOST CALIFORNIANS PRAY FOR LOUSY WEATHER . . . TO KEEP THIS PLACE FROM BECOMING OVERCROWDED.

THERE IS A CHANCE THAT THE DOLPHIN MAY GO BACK IN FLOYD'S LIVING ROOM. THERE IS A GIANT OLD TANK ON THE BACK LOT HERE AT MGM. ESTHER WILLIAMS* USED TO USE IT FOR UNDERWATER SHOTS. I MAY HAVE FIGURED OUT A WAY TO BUILD THE FLOYD LIVING ROOM OVER THE TANK. WE ARE IN THE MIDST OF TRYING TO GET APPROVAL FROM ALL OF THE VARIOUS AND SUNDRY ORGANIZATIONS AND AGENCIES THAT CONTROL THE USE OF MAMMALS IN FILM. WE HAVE A CHANCE.

IF I THINK HOW LITTLE TIME IS LEFT BEFORE SHOOTING STARTS . . . I START TO HYPERVENTILATE . . . SO I WON'T THINK ABOUT IT.

I AM SORRY TO HEAR THAT YOU MAY NOT BE ABLE TO COME OUT TO SEE SOME OF THE SHOOTING. IT WOULD BE NOTHING LESS THAN A THRILL FOR ME TO SHOW YOU WHAT IS GOING ON HERE. I HOPE YOU CAN WORK SOMETHING OUT. IF NOTHING ELSE . . . IT SHOULD GIVE YOU

---

* Esther Williams starred in many famous MGM aquatic extravaganzas in the fifties.

SOME SENSE OF SATISFACTION TO SEE ALL OF THE CHAOS
YOU HAVE CAUSED.

ACC86 of 84 Jan 3

Just received the cover of "Ascent
to Orbit" from John Wiley. Looks
stunning--gold and silver foil,
full-color photo of the Earth in
space. And large format with 100,000
words. Not to mention 2001 and 2010
all across the top.

Closing this file at 11 p.m., two
hours after my usual bedtime. But
our Washington ambassador, Ernest
Corea, is in town and I've been having dinner with him. They're planning a bash for the Arthur Clarke
Foundation on April 27. It looks
more and more unlikely that I shall
survive to get further west.

PH66. JANUARY 4, 1984

I RECIEVED A SERIES OF DELIGHTED NOTES FROM THE IN-
FOMEDIA PEOPLE ... REJOICING OVER THE FACT
THAT YOU "MADE IT ON LINE" ... THIS MORNING OUR
TIME. DID YOU CALL DIRECTLY FROM SRI LANKA TO CALI-

FORNIA . . . OR HAVE YOU FOUND A LOCAL ACCESS NUM-
BER. IF THE LATTER IS TRUE . . . I AM DELIGHTED . . . AND
I HOPE WE CAN START TO USE THAT SYSTEM. IF IT IS NOT
TRUE . . . I WILL KEEP HARASSING THEM.

THEY HAVE OPENED A NEW ACTIVITY . . . IT IS CALLED
"FUTURES PLANNING" OR SOMETHING LIKE THAT. IT IS
FOR YOU AND ME . . . AND FOR CARL SAGAN . . . WHO IS
JOINING THEIR PROGRAM IN THE NEXT DAY OR TWO.
HOAGLAND ASKED THAT YOU LOG IN AND CHECK THAT AC-
TIVITY. THERE IS A VERY IMPORTANT CONFERENCE THAT
THEY ARE HOLDING . . . I THINK IN WASHINGTON THIS
WEEKEND . . . FILLED WITH CELESTIAL CELEBRITIES LIKE
YOURSELF, AND THE DEPUTY SECRETARY GENERAL OF
THE UNITED NATIONS . . . AS WELL AS RALPH NADER, AND
I THINK WALTER CRONKITE. I THINK THEY WANT TO KNOW
IF YOU ARE INTERESTED. I TOLD THEM I WOULD FOWARD
THIS INFORMATIOON TO YOU. I HAVE.

AS FAR AS THE REST OF THIS DAY GOES . . . JUST ABOUT
EVERYTHING THAT COULD GO WRONG . . . HAS GONE
WRONG. A FILM IS COMPRISED OF HUNDREDS OF THESE
DAYS. I HATE THEM ALL.

ACC87 of 84 Jan 4

It has been a complicated day, as the
house has been closed for fumigation
and I've only just now been able to
get back to the keyboard. The Ceylon
cockroach has been known to carry
off small children, and as we have a
new baby in the house, we are taking
no chances. Still, I feel a bit
guilty as the mail brought a clip-

ping from the New York Times headed
"dear nasa" from a great-great-
grandson of archie, i quote "a
roachs reach must exceed its grasp
or whats a heaven for once we have
colonized the galley on mr begg s
fine new space station we will aim
for the home of our ancestors on the
star . . . which human children
call beetlejuice." Well, I hope
we've decolonised our galley today.

ACC88 of 84 Jan 4

Happy we may have dolphins after
all.

PH68. JANUARY 11, 1984

THIS IS SOMETHING OF A GOOD NEWSFLASH. THE DOLPHIN
MAY IN FACT BE ALIVE AND WELL, AND SWIMMING IN THE
ESTHER WILLIAMS' TANK AT MGM. I THINK I FOUND A WAY
TO MAKE IT WORK . . . AND MGM IS AGREEABLE TO SPEND
THE MONEY. (IT IS AMAZING WHAT HAPPENS AT A STUDIO
WHEN A DIRECTOR FLAILS AWAY ON THE CHAIRMAN OF THE
BOARD'S CARPET AND CRIES.) WE ARE GOING AHEAD WITH
THE PLANS NOW.

ACC93 of 84 Jan 11

Did you know they've detected a 100 km high and 200 km wide plume on Europa?! (Allan Cook, National Research Council of Canada's Herzberg Institute of Astrophysics) The reference in NRC's "Science Dimension 1983/5" mentions "2010" and has a lovely description of Europa as "the solar system's best maintained skating rink." They think the plume may be a vent through cracked ice.

Today I had a letter from Nature asking me to comment on the Reynolds et al. paper "On the Habitability of Europa" (which I presume JPL has shown you) with particular reference to 2010. Would love to do so if I wasn't sinking under my mail etc. load.

_____

ACC94 of 84 Jan 12

Delighted to hear about the dolphin situation. Squeak, click, click...

_____

PH69. JANUARY 13, 1984

THIS IS FRIDAY THE THIRTEENTH HERE. YOURS IS ALREADY
PAST . . . SO IF YOU ARE ABLE TO RECIEVE THIS FILE . . .
NOTHING THAT DIRE COULD HAVE HAPPENED TO YOU.

THE PRELIMINARY TESTS LOOK FAIRLY GOOD. MORE THAN
ANYTHING . . . I AM TRYING TO ACHIEVE A LOOK FOR THIS
FILM AND THESE SETS THAT IS DIFFERENT FROM WHAT
PEOPLE HAVE SEEN BEFORE. THERE IS A CHANCE THAT IT
WILL ACTUALLY WORK.

FEDERAL AND STATE INSPECTORS ARE HOVERING AROUND
THE ESTHER WILLIAMS TANK . . . TRYING TO DETERMINE IF
IT IS SUITABLE FOR OUR DOLPHIN. IT TURNS OUT THAT YOU
HAVE TO BRING OVER THREE DOLPHINS SO THAT NO ONE
WILL GET LONELY. I TOLD THEM THAT THREE DOLPHINS IS
FINE WITH ME . . . AS LONG AS ONLY ONE IS IN THE
HOUSE. THE DOLPHINS CAN CHOOSE AMONG THEMSELVES
. . . AS TO WHICH ONE BECOMES A MOVIE STAR.

ACC96 of 84 Jan 14

I feel very happy--after weeks of
hunting I've located and identified
eight of the twelve comsats in my
sky, though I can only get good TV
from three (two Russian, one Indian). I've also been able to peek at
Intelsat newsfeeds. No wonder I've
had no time to think about writing
. . . but doubtless my subconscious
is bubbling away. The President's*
just asked for a copy of "2010," so

---

* President J. R. Jayawardene

I'll send over the boxed Phantasia
edition. I can't imagine how he'll
ever have time to read it . . . Stay
tuned.

ACC97 of 84 Jan 16

Let the President down today. Last
night he called to say he'd started
on "2010" and could I come to lunch.
Said, "Fine--I'll wear my national
dress." When I turned up, President
and Mrs P cried "????" I had to confess that I'd had a nosebleed just
before leaving, which left me looking as if I'd just come from the
operating theatre, and so had to
make a quick change to shirt and
slacks. Too bad, as I'd hoped to im-
press the other guests (Senators
Eagleton and Mark Hatfield--who
wish the movie good luck. N.B.
tickets for the Washington pre-
miere. . . .) Also David Hopper,
World Bank Vice President, who seems
to know all about the Arthur Clarke
Centre . . . encouraging.

PH70. JANUARY 17, 1984

I RECIEVED A LETTER FROM SCOTT MEREDITH. HE WAS PO-
LITELY COMPLAINING ABOUT THE FACT THAT I WILL NOT
ALLOW PHOTOGRAPHS AND DESIGNS OF THE FILM TO BE
PUBLISHED BEFORE THE FILM OPENS. HE SAID THAT THIS
WOULD DRASTICALLY CUT DOWN THE POSSIBILITY OF TIE-
IN BOOKS . . . WHICH WOULD HAVE TO BE PUBLISHED IN
NOVEMBER. BEFORE I RESPOND TO HIM . . . I WANTED TO
LET YOU KNOW MY FEELINGS. I REALIZE HOW HELPFUL
THOSE BOOKS CAN BE TO A FILM . . . AND I ALSO KNOW
HOW PROFITABLE THEY CAN BE. HOWEVER, MY FIRST AND
ONLY PRIORITY IS THIS FILM . . . AND I CANNOT ALLOW
. . . UNDER ANY CIRCUMSTANCES . . . CERTAIN DESIGNS
AND PHOTOGRAPHS TO BE RELEASED BEFORE THE FILM IS
IN THE THEATERS. THERE ARE SOME VISUALS THAT I WILL
ALLOW. IF THEY WOULD SUFFICE . . . THEN I CAN GO OVER
EACH AND EVERY ONE OF THEM WHEN THE TIME COMES.
AS FOR ALL OF THE VISUALS . . . I AM AFRAID I WILL NOT
BUDGE. I HOPE YOU UNDERSTAND.

THINGS ARE PROGRESSING HERE IN THEIR NORMAL
CHAOS. ROY SCHEIDER HAS ARRIVED. I AM TESTING AL-
MOST DAILY. KEEP FEBRUARY 6TH IN YOUR HEAD. IT IS
THE DATE WE BEGIN IN EARNEST. GOD HELP US ALL.

ACC98 of 84 Jan 17

I agree completely with you--as far
as the movie is concerned, you're
the boss. But I'm sure some compro-
mise can be arranged as you suggest.
Scott and Del Rey have a point and it
would be a pity not to exploit the
enormous advance interest as far as

possible . . . especially as the paperback comes out the month you start shooting. (Have you seen the beautiful publicity?)

Look out for spies from Starlog. I have information that Kerry O'Quinn is attempting to infiltrate the studio, disguised as Jabba the Hutt, or possibly the Rancor (whichever is more inconspicuous).

PH71. JANUARY 19, 1984

A PACKAGE HAS JUST BEEN MAILED TO YOU. I SENT IT REGULAR AIRMAIL . . . AS THAT IS WHAT STEVE SAID IS THE MOST EFFICIENT WAY. THIS PACKAGE CONTAINS A MODEST GIFT FROM ME TO YOU . . . AS WELL AS A MINOR ITEM CALLED THE SCREENPLAY. I WANT YOU TO KNOW THAT I WILL BE IN A CONSTANT STATE OF NAUSEA UNTIL I GET YOUR REACTION. I KNOW THAT IT CANNOT BE AS GOOD AS EVERYBODY SAYS IT IS . . . AND I AM SURE YOU WILL TELL ME EXACTLY WHY IT ISN'T. IT IS FILLED WITH TYPOGRAPHICAL ERRORS. I DID NOT TYPE IT . . . IT IS NOT MY SPELLING, SO FOR GOD'S SAKE DON'T YELL AT ME FOR THAT. IT IS CONSTANTLY BEING UPDATED, AS ALL SCREENPLAYS ARE . . . SO SOME OF THE TECHNICAL DETAILS THAT SHOULD OBVIOUSLY BE CORRECTED HAVE BEEN CORRECTED IN BLUE PAGES THAT ARE NOT OUT YET. I NEVER LIVE UP TO MY EXPECTATIONS . . . SO I AM NEVER HAPPY WITH MY WORK. HOWEVER, I CAN SAY TO YOU THAT MORE THAN ANYTHING ELSE . . . I HAVE TRIED DESPERATELY TO PRESERVE YOUR VISION AND CONCEPT . . . WHILE MAKING THE ALTERATIONS THAT ARE NECESSARY TO TURN A BOOK INTO A FILM. I USE THE TERM "ALTERATIONS" INTENTION-

ALLY. THIS IS YOUR SUIT, OF YOUR DESIGN. I AM NOTHING
MORE THAN A TAILOR . . . TRYING TO FIT IT TO A DIFFER-
ENT BODY. MORE THAN ANYONE ELSE IN THE WORLD . . . I
HOPE YOU ARE PLEASED WITH WHAT YOU READ. NEXT
CHRISTMAS . . . IF YOU AND STANLEY ARE NOT EMBAR-
RASSED BY WHAT YOU SEE . . . I WILL NOT HAVE WASTED
TWO YEARS OF MY LIFE

AS REDUNDANT AS THIS SOUNDS . . . PLEASE REMEMBER
YOUR PROMISE OF CONFIDENTIALITY. THIS PACKAGE IS
FOR YOUR EYES ONLY.

ACC99 of 84 Jan 20

Looking forward very much to your
package containing screenplay and
enormous bribe to say how wonderful
it is. I'll of course hide it from
prying eyes in the safety deposit
box I reserve for those books
curiously called curious.

With luck it should be here in seven
to ten days. The quickest and safest
way is by courier.

Seriously, I look forward very much
to reading it and will give my reaction within 24 hours of receipt.

I don't think I ever actually saw a
complete screenplay of "2001"--if
indeed a final, definitive version
exists. I'd challenge anyone to
script the "Star Gate" sequence.
That would be a nice little exercise

for the Famous Filmmakers' Correspondence School.

ACC100 of 84 Jan 12

I've received an extraordinary report, just submitted to the University of California Press, with the
mind-boggling title: "The Los
Alamos Conference on Interstellar
Migration." (It gives "2010" as a
reference!) Quite apart from such
interesting ideas as mining the sun,
it contains some fascinating an-
thropological titbits about the
settlement of this planet, and what
human beings can do in the way of
population explosion when they
really try. (It mentions an Afghan
camel driver--"who surely holds a
special place in the history of
human reproduction"--who not only
had a second family by a daughter,
but then fathered eight more children by a grand-daughter. Just imagine trying to work out that
genealogy; I hope this sort of thing
isn't necessary in space colonies.
Life will be complicated enough anyway.

ACC103 of 84 Jan 26

Typing this just after hearing President Reagan announce a permanent manned space station. A good omen, I hope . . .

Dr Ray Reynolds (NASA Ames, Moffett Field, 94035) has just sent me his latest paper "On the Habitability of Europa," which gives "2010" as a reference. It's highly technical but you might like to contact him; I'm sure he'd be thrilled.

ACC106 of 84 Jan 31

Well, I won't be meeting President Reagan--the China trip and election campaign rule it out. We're now waiting for the V.P. to confirm a date, and are back in April again. . . . I'll certainly be glad when it's settled, which hopefully will be very soon now. At least April will pose no problems.

ACC107 of 84 Feb 1

"1984: Spring"* just arrived--very handsome! Get a copy from Judy. Did

---

* My latest collection of essays. Rush out and buy it.

you ever order those copies of the
Easton "Satellite Handbook"?

ACC108 of 84 Feb 2

Do you realise that during the next
few days the Shuttle crew will be
performing, for the first time, what
we showed in "2001"--a non-tethered
EVA? (The very first EVA, of course,
was Alexei's*: incidentally, did I
send you the photos of us together at
Star Village?)

ACC110 of 84 Feb ?4?

Get the December Astronomy. It has
an article about Europan life, with
some nice illos. No mention of
"2010," tho!

Hurrah--the Shuttle's off! Now for
the tetherless EVA . . . there
should be some exciting echoes of
"2001" on TV soon.

Hey, what date is the April launch??
We might be there.

---

* Alexei Leonov. See note on page 3.

Just had a call from Tod Hawley,* who
may now have contacted you. He's
helping Fred Durant organise the
Arthur Clarke Foundation, which has
just made the first Arthur Clarke
Award--to Carl Sagan!!

PH72. FEBRUARY 4, 1984

JOHN YOUNG WAS ONCE ASKED WHAT IT FELT LIKE JUST
BEFORE THE APOLLO LAUNCH. HE RESPONDED: "YOU'RE
LYING ON YOUR BACK . . . THIRTY-FIVE STORIES IN THE
AIR . . . ON TOP OF SIX MILLION POUNDS OF PARTS AND
FUEL . . . ALL SUBMITTED BY THE LOWEST BIDDER." HERE
I AM. THERE IS NO ONE IN THE STUDIO. I SPENT MOST OF
THE DAY ALONE ON THE STAGES. THE DISCOVERY POD BAY
IS DARK . . . JUST AS IT WILL BE FOUND BY CURNOW AND
BRAILOVSKY. THE LEONOV IS EMPTY. ONLY THE WORK
LIGHTS ARE ON. YOU FORGET WHEN YOU ARE INSIDE . . .
THAT THE OUTER SKIN IS WOOD AND FLUORESCENT TUBES
. . . COVERED BY A MAZE OF WIRING. THERE ARE MO-
MENTS WHEN YOU ACTUALLY BELIEVE YOU ARE IN AN-
OTHER TIME. THEN YOU SEE A GAP IN THE CEILING . . .
AND THE OLD RAFTERS OF THE SOUND STAGE PEEKING
THROUGH.

I FEEL THE PROP WASH OF 2001 BUFFETING MY LIFE. I AM
NOT MAKING MY FILM. I AM THE CUSTODIAN OF EVERYONE
ELSE'S EXPECTATIONS. THE ONLY COMFORT IS MY TOTAL
CONVICTION IN ONE BELIEF: WHEN A DIRECTOR PUTS THE

---

* Special assistant to the Arthur C. Clarke Foundation of the United
States, which was set up in Washington, D.C., in May 1984 to pro-
mote development in communications and computers in the Third
World (with particular reference to the Arthur C. Clarke Center in
Sri Lanka).

FILM TOGETHER . . . WHEN YOU SPLICE ALL OF THE ART-
FUL PERFORMANCES . . . ALL OF THE ENDLESS DOLLY
SHOTS . . . ALL OF THE SPECIAL EFFECTS . . . ALL OF THE
CAREFUL BACKLIGHTING . . . WHEN YOU ADD ALL OF THEM
UP . . . YOU HAVE THE STORY . . . NOTHING MORE AND
NOTHING LESS. MAKING A FILM IS LIKE PAINTING AN ENOR-
MOUS MURAL. YOU SPEND EACH DAY WORKING ON ONE
SMALL PANEL. IT IS ONLY WHEN YOU ARE DONE . . . DO
YOU GET TO SEE IF YOU HAVE PUT TWO EYES ON THE SAME
SIDE OF A PERSON'S NOSE. MY SALVATION IN THIS CASE IS
THE FACT THAT I AM STANDING ON THE FOUNDATION OF
YOUR REMARKABLE CONCEPT. IT IS YOUR STORY THAT
WILL PREVAIL . . . IF IT CAN SURVIVE MY LACK OF TALENT.

I SAT THERE TODAY . . . IN THE EMPTY SETS . . . SAYING
OUT LOUD: "WHAT HAVE I FORGOTTEN? WHAT WOULD
THE REALLY SPECIAL TALENTS LIKE KUBRICK SEE THAT I
CAN'T SEE NOW? WHAT IS GOING TO COME BACK AND
HAUNT ME NEXT CHRISTMAS?" I DON'T HAVE THE AN-
SWERS. I DO POSSESS THE DEMONIC PASSION TO HAVE
YOU SEE THIS FILM NEXT DECEMBER . . . AND FEEL THAT
SOMEHOW OR OTHER . . . YOUR AMAZING GLIMPSE INTO
THE PROCESS HAS BEEN TRANSLATED PROPERLY.

ACC113 of 84 Feb 6

Nice timing, Peter--the screenplay
arrived this morning . . . I felt
like playing a few tricks on you--
like a message from my secretary
saying that I was last seen heading
for the airport carrying a gun. But
being the day it is and the delicate
condition you are in I'll say right
away that it's a splendid job and you
have brilliantly chiselled out the
basic elements of the novel, besides
adding quite a few of your own. I
laughed--and cried--in all the
right places.

At the same time you have left enough
loose ends to make everyone rush out
and buy the book. . . .

During the next few days I'll carefully re-read it (naturally the
first time was a hypersonic skim)
and doubtless will find a few nits to
pick, and some suggestions you can
take or leave. But I doubt if they
will be important.

Now--here's a weirdie for you to
mull over. . . . My brother has
just sent me a clipping about Helen
Mirren, who I must confess I'd not
heard of before. It refers to her ex-
boy friend, "the Duke of Kent's
White Russian cousin, painter
George Galitzine."

Well, when I was six or seven, we had
a Russian lady staying in the house

where I was born. She was Princess
Galitzine.

All I can say at the moment is EEEK.

Finally: another strange thing happened today which made me feel very
sad. Some visitors brought a personal letter from dear old Bucky
Fuller,* saying, "If I live long
enough I will attempt to again visit
you . . . Does your new bigger house
have the monkeys?" Well, Bucky and
monkeys are gone, and I weep for them
all.

ACC114 of 84 Feb 7

A lot has happened since I spoke to
you this a.m. Cosmonaut Lyakov--who
was lucky to get back from that last
mission--wants to visit the Arthur
Clarke Centre at the end of the
month. A nice guy (like all of them).
Took him for a ride in the Hovercraft
last visit; this time I'll tease him
with "2010" . . .

The only Englishman I've always
wanted to meet and never have is also
coming here--Captain Scott's† son

---

* R. Buckminster Fuller. Bucky is best known as the inventor of the
geodesic dome, and as an architect/philosopher has inspired at least
three generations of young Americans.
† Robert Falcon Scott, RN, who led the expedition to the South Pole
in 1912 only to discover that Amundsen had beaten him to it. Scott
and all his companions died on the return journey.

Sir Peter. (See my best story "Transit of Earth" in May--probably the first and last time Omni will reprint from Playboy. . . .)

I've been asked to keynote a communications conference in New Delhi 1 March (Mrs Gandhi presiding). Would rather like to, but I'm doing exactly the same thing in Saudi the same week.

Do you know where I can buy a good cloning kit?

At least I had an evening off--took everyone to "Lost Ark." Just as enjoyable as first time round; the music brought back memories of writing "2010"--I played it all the time. . . .

Hope all going well--will call as usual at 7:45 my time.

Dialogue 28 of 84 Feb 7

THIS IS HYAMS. STEVE BROUGHT YOUR RESPONSE TO THE STAGE FOR ME. I CANNOT BEGIN TO TELL YOU HOW IT MADE ME FEEL. I AM GRATEFUL AND A BIT MORE THAN RELIEVED. I AM SURE THAT WHEN YOU READ IT MORE CAREFULLY . . . THERE WILL BE COMMENTS . . . HOWEVER, THIS FIRST RESPONSE . . . BEFORE YOUR HEADMASTER MODE TAKES OVER . . . IS THE MOST CHERISHED MOMENT I HAVE HAD SINCE I SAID I WAS FOOLISH ENOUGH TO DO THIS FILM. I THANK YOU.

APPENDIX I
2010:
FROM NOVEL TO SCRIPT

FROM NOVEL TO SCRIPT

In adapting Arthur C. Clarke's novel to film, writer/director Peter Hyams made several significant thematic and structural changes. The first was the elimination of the ill-fated voyage of the Chinese spacecraft *Tsien*. Hyams felt that seeing the surface of Europa early on (as happens in the novel) gives away much of the mystery so critical to the story. Therefore in the film, an unmanned probe is sent from the *Leonov* because sensors have detected signs of life on Europa. The viewer watches the probe descend to investigate, and just as the surface comes into focus, the probe is mysteriously destroyed. Not until the end of the film do we see life on Europa and realize that it is fostered and protected by whoever or whatever lies behind the monolith.

In the novel, Clarke spends a great deal of time getting the crew of the *Leonov* to Jupiter. Hyams bypasses this long travel sequence by beginning the film with *Leonov* already in its approach to the Jovian system. This dramatic device keeps the pace brisk without sacrificing story content.

Another major change written into the film by Hyams is political. At the outset of the film, America and Russia are moments away from nuclear war, and the estrangement between the two countries is the source of much of the suspense and the tension in the film. This new note is "set up" in the opening scene between Floyd and Moisevitch. Their deep friendship, so prominent in the novel, has been eliminated from the film, where neither knows nor trusts the other. Moisevitch still proposes a joint mission to rendezvous with the abandoned *Discovery,* and Floyd ultimately accepts for the same reasons: the Russians have the ship ready to make the voyage, and the Americans have the technical wherewithal to reactivate *Discovery*—which will crash into Io before the Americans reach her if they wait until *Discovery II* is available. It is in this first scene that we learn of the threat of war.

MOISEVITCH: This is very bad business in South America . . . very bad . . .

FLOYD: We didn't start it.

MOISEVITCH: Come now, Dr. Floyd. We are scientists . . . you and I. Our governments are enemies. We are not.

The theme of community in science versus the factionalism of politics is constantly echoed throughout the film. Once aboard the *Leonov,* the Americans are treated like nothing more than unwelcome guests, but as the voyage progresses, political differences are set aside and the two crews become one in the face of the awesome events unfolding before them. Contrasted to this evolving unity is the growing hostility between the two governments on Earth. In fact, things get so bad that the two crews are ordered to separate and are given different flight instructions for the return home.

With this added political overtone, *2010*'s climactic ending takes on even larger and more meaningful dimensions. The message sent to Earth rings louder and truer in the face of an impending war, and ultimately we are left with a hopeful feeling about our future.

FLOYD (v.o.) You can tell your children of the day when everyone looked up . . . and realized that we are only tenants on this world. We have been given a new lease . . . and a warning from the landlord.

Thus Hyams' vision is more human-orientated and remains entrenched in the twentieth century, whereas Clarke's novel takes a more cosmic view of the human race, much in keeping with the themes of his earlier novels such as *Childhood's End*.

Hyams also eliminated Bowman's lengthy journey through the star-gate and solar system. The reasons for this are several. First, there is limited time for a movie to tell its story. Second, this sojourn is difficult to translate onto the screen, and Hyams desperately wanted a film accessible to audiences of all ages. Bowman's farewells to his mother and to his former wife remain. And, of course, he still delivers the critical speech to Floyd warning him that the spacecraft and crews must leave the vicinity of Jupiter. However, his warning comes during the critical time when war has been declared on Earth, and the two crews have separated. In the novel they are given two weeks, in the movie two days, thus creating a situation whereby Floyd must quickly convince a skeptical Captain Kirbuk that the Americans and the

Soviets must disobey orders and escape together. She refuses to believe him, and only when she learns that the giant two-kilometer monolith has vanished does she come to understand that Floyd is genuinely onto something.

In the film, Floyd's character takes a more active and heroic role in the mission: not only does he insist on going, but he also names his crew. In the novel, Clarke's Floyd is more passive: "Four men had died, and one had disappeared out there among the moons of Jupiter. There was blood on his hands and he did not know how to wash them clean." Hyams' Floyd knows how: "I want to go. Good men died up there . . . and I sent them. I have no choice." Floyd's subtle character change reflects the cinematic necessity of a stronger lead.

The love between the Floyds and their pain of separation is more acutely demonstrated in the film than in the novel. For instance, Hyams made their son Christopher five instead of two, so that he would have some idea as to where and for how long his father was going. In addition at an emotional moment in the film not present in Clarke's novel, Floyd looks in on his sleeping son and gives him an anguished look of farewell. Although Floyd sends messages home, in both the book and the film, those in the film often contain more than just the personal material described in the novel. For instance, Floyd's first message to Caroline, which is not taken from the novel, incorporates a theme which seems to be one of Hyams' statements in the movie.

FLOYD (v.o.): . . . In this brief time up here . . . I've been given a glimpse of things I will never understand, and I will always be affected by . . . Presidents and Premiers should see Jupiter from this proximity. Then they would all realize how petty and futile it is for us not to live together.

In another departure from the novel, Hyams has made Chandra an American instead of an Indian, in order to keep the political nature of the movie more clearly focused on the two superpowers. Hyams also has dovetailed the crucial test of Hal and the decay of Jupiter into one exciting climax. Once again the state of war lends more significance to the story because the crews can only escape death by disobeying their governments and working together for mutual survival.

The tension of whether Hal will fire *Discovery*'s rockets or not is heightened in the film by having Chandra finally break down and tell him the truth. In the novel Chandra persists in the lie. The dialogue in the film best sums up Hyams' reason for changing this story point.

HAL: Thank you for telling me the truth.

CHANDRA: You deserve it.

Unlike in the novel, Brailovsky is killed while investigating the surface of the monolith. His death serves to emphasize the final warning—stay away from Europa—while acting as a catalyst to bring the two crews together.

Hyams also changed the life-form on Europa. In the novel, Clarke describes creatures that are capable of thought but physically similar to a lower form of terrestrial sea-life. In the film the "Europans" have been eliminated in favor of a more traditional and familiar image—plants. Thus we witness a more earth-like evolution taking place as opposed to the birth of an alien civilization. Clarke jumps ahead twenty thousand years in describing the growth of the Europans:

> The Europans would be surprised to know with
> what intensity and baffled wonder that the black
> monolith was also studied by the minds behind
> those moving lights. . . . For until the time is ripe,
> the monolith will permit no contact. When that
> time comes . . . the monolith may change its
> strategy. It may—or it may not—choose to re-
> lease the entities who slumber within it, so that
> they can bridge the gulf between the Europans,
> and the race to which they once held allegiance.
> And it may be that no such bridge is possible,
> and that two such alien forms of consciousness
> can never coexist. If this is so then only one of
> them can inherit the solar system. Which one it
> will be, not even the Gods know—yet.

The film does not make so great a leap through
time. Instead, the closing shot is a long pan across the
new surface of Europa. The plant life has grown to
brilliant greens. The ice has melted into a new ocean,
and the new sun shines in the distance. As we continue to pan we see the monolith jutting from the new
sea. This image conveys the feeling of genesis, under
the watchful presence of the monolith, much like the
Dawn of Man in *2001*. Thus, the closing shots give us
a glimpse of the future while recalling the past. The
corresponding images from the film's classic prede-
cessor are conjured up with the telling image of the
plant-entities reaching out to touch the monolith.

Hyams' contribution to *2010* then, has been one necessitated by the nature of the film medium. The
tighter construction of the film—especially the dra-

matic tension resulting from the dovetailing of HAL's complete rehabilitation and the escape from Jupiter—contributes much to making *2010* a dynamic and moving film of the eighties. The emphasis on the US-Soviet conflict brings down to earth Clarke's cosmic ideas of a peaceful universe. Finally, Hyams has fleshed out the characters of the book, and with the help of the actors portraying those characters on the screen, he has given movie-going audiences human heroes to whom they can relate. Clarke's ultimate hero, however, is the intelligence behind the monolith which, on the screen, can only be represented by the black slab accompanied by the characteristic opening notes to the Zarathustra theme.

—Steven Jongeward
Los Angeles, California
August, 1984

APPENDIX II
MITE FOR MORONS *

---

* I am afraid that this chapter will amply demonstrate the truth of Clarke's 69th Law, viz., "Reading computer manuals without the hardware is as frustrating as reading sex manuals without the software." In both cases the cure is simple though usually very expensive.

INTRODUCTION

Needed: 1. Kaypro Computer.
2. Hayes Smartmodem (or equivalent), connected to international dialing phone.
3. A drive disk containing MITE and WordStar programs.
4. B drive disk to save and edit messages.
5. Printer (optional but highly desirable for hard copy).

Notes:

Familiarity with the basic WordStar instructions (editing, copying, formating, etc.) is assumed.

The MITE program allows one to send files over the normal phone circuits at a speed set by the modem. The normal speed is 300 baud (bits per second), which is equivalent to about 40 characters or 8 words per second. This means that it takes about a minute to transmit a double-spaced page. Much higher speeds are possible over good circuits.

In normal operation, one station originates a call (ORG mode) while the other receives (ANS mode). The receiving station can be unattended as long as it is properly set up and connected to the phone line. (One disadvantage of the system is that a station in ANS ties up the circuit; incoming phone calls cannot be made to that number.)

If both stations are attended, it is also possible for the operators to "converse" with each other as fast as they can type, as with the now obsolete teleprinter. However, this is expensive in terms of phone time, so as much material as possible should be preloaded for fast autotransmission.

Such real-time conversations can also be saved for subsequent editing and printing if the computer has been specially instructed in advance (CAPTURE mode). Otherwise they will be lost when the circuit is broken.

To sum up:

The originator opens a file, types and edits his message, and then saves it on Disk B. (Disk A could be used, but it is best to reserve that for the command files.)

He then exits from WordStar and runs the MITE command. A menu then appears on the screen, and he selects the items which will permit transmission of the file. Although dialing can be done manually, it is much more convenient to have the required number already loaded in a special (PAR) file so that dialing is automatic (and accurate!).

Here are the instructions in detail.

TO SEND A FILE

1. Loading the phone number of the other party's machine.

When the A prompt appears, type MITE (and of course press the Return key—this is assumed from now on). If you were in WordStar, exit first by typing X.

The MITE Menu will now appear. (It's the Main Menu only, and there are several Sub-Menus.) Although it looks very confusing, as in the case of a Chinese restaurant only half a dozen items will ever concern you; all the others can be ignored, and some need be dealt with only once.

The first thing to be done is to give the machine the number you want to call. Suppose you wish to communicate with Bill Sykes at 001-333-3333. His number can be permanently stored by opening up a Parameter (Par) file as follows.

Once the Main Menu is on the screen, press P.

The Parameter Menu will appear: the *only* item

that concerns you is N. Press that: the message "Enter new phone number" appears.

Before you do this, there is one complication. Some automatic dialing systems require a letter *p* before the number. You will have to check this with your local telecommunications people. Then type 001-333-3333 *or* p001-333-3333, as the case may be, and press the Return key.

Now press X to get back to the Main Menu. The number has been saved—but hasn't got a name attached to it yet.

Press S. The instruction "Enter file name" will appear. Type BILL or SYKES or any other file name you'll remember easily. (And Return, of course; from now on this will be assumed.)

That's it: Bill's number has now been stored once and for all. . . . Any number of names and numbers, up to the capacity of the disk, can be stored in this way for automatic dialing. You will see them all in the directory of the A disk, like this: SYKES.PAR, BILL.PAR, etc. (If you try to *look* at these files, by the TYPE or D command, you will see the most incredible garbage. But the phone number is tucked away in there somewhere.)

2. Sending a File.

You are now ready to send the file on Disk B. Call it Ishmael . . .

Switch on the modem! (Surprising how often this is forgotten the first few times.) No one can call you now; if they try the modem will make strange noises. You may be able to switch off in time to take the call if you have not yet started to transmit.

You should have the Main Menu on the screen. Press L.

"Enter file name" will appear. Type BILL or SYKES or whomever you wish to send to. (There is no need to type the .PAR as well.)

Press G. Dialing will start.

If the line is bad, or Bill's modem is not in ANSwer mode, you will see

> No carrier detected

Press ESC, which will take you back to the main menu. Try G again. And again . . . until there's an answer, or it's obvious that Bill is not on line. In this case switch off the modem.

If Bill's machine is ready to receive, you will see something like

> Carrier detected
> AT
> CONNECT
> MITE . . . Copyright . . .
> Remote Trigger Character = 12 H

The machine is now waiting for your instructions; you have to tell it to RECEIVE the file, and your machine to SEND it.

Type CTRL R (the Ctrl *key,* not the letters Ctrl!). This means "control remote" and does just that, as is indicated by the reply: Remote command?

Now type: DRIVE B:

This will ensure that your file is stored on B: disk. If you don't do this—or type B; instead of B:—it will automatically go on A and Bill may overlook it, as he'll be expecting it on B.

Now type CTRL R (this has to be done every time you send a new instruction) followed by RECV ISH-MAEL.

Bill's machine is now fully expecting your file, so you have to tell your machine to send it. Type CTRL K, which means loc(k)al control as opposed to remote control.

Then type SEND B:ISHMAEL.

Your machine will think it over for a second; then you will see the message

ATTEMPTING TO SYNCHRONIZE

followed by

SENDING B:ISHMAEL

Then dots will appear at intervals of about five seconds, advancing slowly across the screen. Each dot represents two lines of text, so you can see the progress of the transmission.

Occasionally the letter R may appear. This means that there is an electrical glitch somewhere, but the transmission will continue after a pause. There may be several RRRRs before it resumes.

If there is a U—that means disaster; the transmission has been aborted, and you will have to try again. Even if there was only one letter still to go, there will be *nothing* in Bill's file Ishmael, even though the name will appear in his directory!

When the whole file has been transmitted, there will be a message:

ATTEMPTING TO SYNCHRONIZE
ALL FILES SENT
RESUMING LINK

TO RECEIVE A FILE

In this case the procedure is much simpler, as you merely have to put your machine in ANSwer mode, and all the work will be done at the other end.

Once again you start with the Main Menu—and make sure you have plenty of space on your B disk for any possible message.

Press P to get the Parameter Menu.

The *only* entry that concerns you is

R – Role (ANS/ORG) = ORG

This means that the machine is now set to originate a message; it is known as the default mode because this is what will be done *unless you give specific instructions to the contrary.* (There are countless default modes in MITE and WordStar for such matters as margins, paper length, page numbering, set for reasonable values so you won't have to insert them every time you call up a program.)

Press R.

ORG will instantly switch on ANS (and back again if you press R once more; this is known as toggling).

Press X to return to the Main Menu.

Press G for Go.

The screen will read:

Awaiting incoming call—abort with ESC

(If it doesn't, you've forgotten to switch on the modem!)

The machine is now waiting for a message and you can go away and leave it. When a message does come through, the modem will make various noises, and the screen display will announce when transmission is complete. Unless you want to get into a real-time conversation with the sender, you can go into Word-Star and look at the new file you have just received, and if necessary edit it in the normal way before printing it out.

About the Authors

ARTHUR C. CLARKE was born in England in 1917. He is the author of almost fifty books, some twenty million copies of which have been printed in over thirty languages. He has been awarded the gold medal of the Franklin Institute, the Kalinga Prize, the AAAS-Westinghouse science writing prize, the Bradford Washburn Award, and the Hugo, Nebula, and John W. Campbell Memorial awards—all three of which were won by his novel *Rendezvous with Rama*. In 1968 he shared an Oscar nomination with Stanley Kubrick for *2001:A Space Odyssey*. His invention of the communications satellite in 1945 has brought him numerous honors. The President of Sri Lanka recently nominated him Chancellor of the University of Moratuwa, near Colombo, Sri Lanka, where he resides.

PETER HYAMS was born on July 26, 1943, the son of a Broadway publicist and the grandson of Sol Hurok, the great impresario.

His professional career began with a stint in news at WCBS-TV in New York. He then landed a post as a Vietnam war correspondent for the network. During his CBS years he began to make documentary films.

He moved to Los Angeles in 1970 and sold his first screenplay, *T. R. Baskin*, to Paramount. He first explored space in the film *Capricorn One*, an intricate story of a space mission that wasn't. He made his maiden voyage to Jupiter with *Outland*. He also wrote and directed the romantic *Hanover Street* and *The Star Chamber*.